My Fathers Prostitute:
Story of a Stolen Childhood

My Fathers Prostitute:
Story of a Stolen Childhood

Steven Whitacre

Steven Whitacre
2014

First Printing: 2014

ISBN 978-1-304-77400-2

www.facebook.com/journeytobpd

Dedication

To my amazing wife, without whom I could never have made the journey.

To my children, who makes the jouney worthwhile.

And to all the men and women still suffering.

Acknowledgements

This book would not have been possible without the efforts of many people. It was truly a community effort to help bring my thoughts together into a coherent mess. To Melanie Vallee for helping me take my power back, Jeanne Gustafson and Kim Young for their awesome editing prowess, Marian Hoyle for helping me believe in myself, and all the incredible people who supported and encouraged me along the way.

1

"Children of tomorrow live in the tears that fall today."

– Black Sabbath, *Children of the Grave*

"Let's play" – two words that delight most children, especially when it is a parent talking to a five-year-old. After all, what child doesn't want to play with their parents? In my case, however, those two words uttered on that sunny afternoon were followed by an event that profoundly changed my life.

Growing up, I think I was pretty much like every other boy in the neighborhood. I played in mud, I rode bikes with friends, I built things. I loved being outside. It was fun there; it was safe. I was a good student, always getting good grades and helping the teacher. In third grade, I even helped the 5th graders with their math. I earned my school letter in elementary school, I played Little League baseball, and ate hot dogs down by the creek. Nobody would ever guess that I had such a deep, dark secret. One that had the potential to completely tear my life apart if it was to be known. It was a secret that I had to protect and keep at all costs.

Growing up, I was forced to have sex with my father. Not once, not twice, not a hundred times, but regularly for years. I can still remember the first time. Where it happened, what led up to it, what was said. I remember the sun shining. I remember the floral print of the bedspread. I could even tell you the number of pillows and what color the pillowcases were that day (they were light blue, if you must know). What I couldn't tell you is why. My mom and sisters weren't home. It was just my father and me, and he had been tickling me. I was five so that didn't seem odd to me. We were just playing around. So when he said "Let's play", I thought it was strange because that's what we were already doing. Then he got serious and told me to take off my clothes. I remember thinking what a strange thing to ask but, being a good son, I did what I was told. It was over in just a few minutes. As he cleaned himself up, I remember wondering what had just happened. It didn't hurt, but I didn't like it, either.

My parents were my whole world, and my father was king. He was an amazing person. He could drive, he could build things, he supported the family. How could anything he did be wrong? So, as confusing as it was, I accepted it.

My family life, with the exception of the abuse, wasn't so bad. I had my older sister to play with since we were only two years apart so I was never really lonely. As a family, we would go out for ice cream in the summer, we would go to fun places like zoos, we would throw open the French doors to the porch and have a bar-b-que. My grandparents lived nearby so we would have big family gatherings on the holidays, and Christmas was always a delight with lots of presents under the tree and a full day or two of festivities. I would help my father in his workshop, building and fixing things, and he would take me along on his trips to the dump, buying McDonalds or getting donuts on the way home. He would frequently go out early on Saturday mornings and pick up warm donuts for us to start our day with. We did things together and seemed like a rather tight-knit family, but things aren't always what they seem.

My father was a large man and had a violent temper. He wasn't somebody you wanted to make angry. You wouldn't know it if you met him on the street because he was very friendly and helpful to strangers and friends. At home, however, he was a different person. Although I have absolutely no recollection of it, he would apparently beat me quite badly. My sister tells me that she remembers times when he would be beating me, and my sisters would be hiding on the other side of the house, crying for it to stop, asking my mother to make it stop, only to be told that she couldn't do anything about it. I learned early not to say "NO" to my father. That just wasn't done for any reason. This, of course, made it a lot easier for him to continue on with the sexual abuse. After all, I knew that if I was to refuse, he would just beat me and do it anyway. So I spared myself the beatings and just submitted.

This continued on and, looking back, I would say that it happened an average of 2-3 times per week. He started out just doing it in his bed. But, soon, that moved to my bed or in the bathroom. I still have vivid memories of lying on the floor with my head next to the toilet, looking up at the toilet bowl and waiting for it to be over. Over time, he would get more and more risky. He would pull into a parking lot and do it on the floor of the van, or he would find a locked room at the church and do it there. It didn't really matter where we were. All he needed was a little privacy and ten minutes. Of course, the never knowing when or where it was going to happen, only that it WAS going to happen sooner or later, kept my brain in a state of constant alertness. Was it going to be here? There? The threat was always there and it kept me on "high alert".

As the years went on, I learned to escape into my head while this was happening. I didn't want to be a part of it so I went somewhere else. It wasn't just the disgust at what was physically happening that made me want to escape. In fact, that was probably easier to deal with than what was going on inside my head. Here was this person that I relied on for everything. He was the person that took care of all of my needs and I *needed* him to ensure my survival. Granted, I probably didn't, but at five-years-old, I didn't have the luxury of hindsight and I was too young to be able to reason though things. I was a captive. Here was this person that was my entire world, doing something to me that I didn't like and didn't want, yet I had to accept it because I didn't feel that I had any choice. I knew there was something wrong about it, but he was my father and he loved me. He wouldn't do me wrong, no matter how *I* felt about it, so it must be okay. After all, he loved me and I trusted him with my life. I had to. Since I couldn't trust him *and* trust my feelings at the same time, I began to not trust myself. This lack of trust in myself, along with the utter powerlessness that I was feeling over the situation, was beginning to form the foundation of how I would live my life for the next 40 years or so.

Looking back, it's really no surprise that I got into drugs and alcohol at a somewhat early age. I was 13 when I first smoked pot, and I can still remember where it was and who I was with. To the best of my knowledge, none of the people I got stoned with that day went on to be hardcore drug users and, in fact, at least one of them went on to have a highly successful academic career. I was also 13 the first time I got drunk. I had found a box of alcohol under the stairs leading to our basement. Some of them were opened already, some were not. I grabbed an unopened bottle of Jack Daniels and took it to school with me on the day of our 8th grade graduation field trip to Great America, and drank it with some friends in the woods behind the school. I ended up drinking about half of the bottle by myself. I remember a friend handing me a cigarette, telling me it would help get me even *more* messed up. So, of course, I smoked it.

At one point, I stumbled into the school bathroom carrying my radio. As I turned to leave, two guys I had never seen walked in and demanded I give the radio to them. They were much bigger than me, but I didn't care. I laughed at them like a drunken clown and left the bathroom. They threatened to beat me up if I didn't give them the radio, but I was full of liquid courage and just didn't give a damn. I guess they weren't expecting that reaction since they stood there staring, their mouths gaping open as I walked out. On the way to the park, I vomited all over the bus and made a spectacle of myself. You think that would have been enough to never drink again. But, for me, it was as if I had found my way home. I really liked the fact that I now had a way to avoid the horror that was reality. I had found a way to escape and I latched onto it with everything I had.

I was hitting puberty and, by this time, I had been forced to havesex with my father somewhere in the neighborhood of 1,000 times. At 2-3 times per week, it was likely well above that by that time, but the actual number doesn't really matter. Needless to say, it was a lot. I was quickly becoming very withdrawn mentally and emotionally, like a hermit crab pulling into its shell when you touch it. I had learned over the previous eight years that love means having to do things you don't want to do. That love means your feelings don't matter. That love was confusing and painful.

But if that was the only thing I learned about love, it all would have made more sense. But love wasn't just about submitting sexually to the desires of the one who had power over me. My father wasn't a monster that would come in the middle of the night to do bad things. He was actually a good guy if you ignored the obvious. No matter what, he always had my back. He always supported me in everything I did, even when he knew it was going to end badly. And when it did, he was there to help pick me up and get me back on my feet. He went to my Little League games, he went to my school plays, he got involved in scouting with me. If you overlooked the fact that he was an incestuous pedophile, he was actually a really good parent. He did everything right according to all of the books and parenting experts. This, of course, made things even more confusing to my young brain. After all, here was this guy who loved me, who actually showed he loved me in all the right ways, using me to quench his own sexual desires. Was that all I was good for? Is that really how relationships are? After all, that was the only thing I knew. It's not like I had any other relationships to indicate otherwise. Deep down, I knew it was wrong. I knew that my friends weren't having sex with their fathers.

But I kept it to myself. I was so beat down emotionally and physically by this point that I didn't have the strength to fight any longer.

Most of my friends had plans for their futures. They had an idea of what they wanted to do with their lives, what schools they wanted to go to, where they might want to live. They had hopes and dreams. Me? Not so much. I was living day-to-day, sometimes minute-to-minute. What might happen five years down the road wasn't on my mind. I was in survival mode…all day, every day. Not knowing when you are going to experience something horrible, only knowing that you will at any time, creates constant stress on the brain. When you know it's coming, you live in a state of constant fear and have no time or room for anything else. When I think back, with the exception of a very short period of time at age ten when I wanted to be a truck driver because I had heard they made $100 a day, which seemed like a ton of money to a ten-year-old in 1978, I really can't think of a single hope or dream that I had. When I was sick, my mother would take me to work with her so she wouldn't have to leave me home alone. She was an attorney who worked out of her own office and I would spend the day lying around in the library, drinking hot chocolate and being bored. When I was old enough, she would have me type up her transcriptions for her. Not exactly a lot of fun for a pre-teen. I decided I never, ever wanted such a boring job. I didn't know WHAT I wanted, only that it wasn't that.

My father would take me to his work, too, but it was for a different reason. He worked in a steel mill and did payroll so he had his own office where he could shut and lock the door. To get there, we had to drive down a long dirt road, past a guard shack where the guard would just wave us through. I hated that road. I knew what it meant was going to happen. I was taken to his office for one thing, and one thing only…sex.

There was one time in his office that stands out. It was the first time that he molested me that ended with me having a shred of hope and a feeling of happiness, thinking "Finally! This is it!" Thinking that the nightmare would end soon. I was around eight-years-old and lying naked on the floor, my father naked on top of me, when we heard the doorknob to his office jiggle. Apparently, he had forgotten to lock the door and it started to open. My father jumped up and ran to the door just as the janitor popped his head in. I will never forget the surprised and shocked look on the janitor's face when he saw what was going on. He quickly apologized and shut the door, but I knew that he saw. I knew he knew what was happening. After all, I had made eye contact with him. I knew he would say something to somebody. He would save me. He *had* to. What person in their right mind could be okay with what was going on?

He never said a word to anybody.

Days went by and nothing changed. I waited. Days turned into weeks. I told myself that it takes time, but that, any day, somebody would come rescue me. But nobody did. Weeks turned into months and I began to give up hope. I came to realize that nobody was coming. Nobody cared. I was just a little boy that wasn't worth saving. Somebody had seen my life and was okay with it. That's just how it was and how it was meant to be. As if I wasn't already emotionally and mentally beat down enough, this was a knockout punch. I was worthless.

That wasn't the only time I thought I might be rescued, or that the horror of my life might come to light. There was the time that my older sister and I were walking to 7-11 with one of the neighborhood kids. We were crossing the street in front of our house when the neighbor told us that our father had told him "If you ever feel too stressed out and need a blow job to relax, let me know and I can help". When he told us that, my heart stopped. My sister didn't believe him, but I knew it was true. I had such mixed emotions. On one hand, he would tell somebody and they would come take our father away. This would end my nightmare and I would be free. On the other hand, he would tell somebody and they would come take our father away and *then* what would we do? I was probably ten or so at the time, but old enough to know that we couldn't make it financially without him. Old enough to believe he was the glue that held our family together, but young enough to not be able to imagine a life without him. It was very confusing. I hated my father, yet I loved him. I feared him, yet I couldn't imagine life without him. With one statement, this neighbor had completely turned my life upside down. I didn't know whether to be happy or afraid, whether to encourage him or to mock him.

So I did nothing. I had learned early on that I couldn't trust my feelings, I couldn't trust anything that came from within me, everything I did and everything I said made things worse…so I did nothing.And the window of opportunity shut. It doesn't appear he ever said anything to anybody or, if he did, they didn't believe him. I continued to wonder why, if all these people knew, nobody cared enough to do anything. Now, you might ask why didn't I just run away? Why didn't *I* say something to somebody? I did, actually. I ran away three times between the ages of 8 and 12. The first time I returned home on my own after getting really hungry, and the other two times I was picked up by the local police. They never once questioned why I had run away. They never once asked me what was wrong. They just returned me to my abuser, no questions asked. Since I don't actually remember what happened after going home, I assume I was beaten pretty badly for running away. I had always been told that the police where there to help, but all they did for me was take me home to be beaten. I was still too young to be able to logically look at the bigger picture so, to me, the police became people that couldn't be trusted. They were on *his* side. And since I couldn't trust my parents and couldn't trust the police, all authority became suspect.

So why didn't I say something to the police in the first place? After all, looking at it with an adult mind, it's not as if they could possibly have had any clue about what was going on if nobody told them. But because I had this total allegiance to my father, I couldn't be the one to turn him in. He was everything to me. He was the only person that I felt actually cared about me so I couldn't turn on him like that. If I did, I would have nobody and would have ruined the life of the one person who cared. It was quite the mindfuck, really. It was certainly much more than any child should have to be worrying about.

People have asked me about my mother. Where was she? Why didn't she step in? She was there. Physically, at least. She was raising four children. I was the second oldest, with two younger sisters, four and six years younger than me. She was going to law school when I was really young, then had her own practice after she graduated. Between the kids and her job, she kept herself busy and was unaware of what was going on, although I suspect she knew something had to be going on. I *know* she knew later and did nothing about it, but I have no idea how early on she knew because when she wasn't working, she was drinking. Apparently a lot. I never knew until she came later and told us that she was an alcoholic, but that would certainly explain why she was never there for us emotionally. It would also explain how she managed to keep her head in the sand while her husband was regularly having sex with her son, practically right in front of her.

So I couldn't trust my mother to save me. To my young and developing mind, she obviously didn't care enough to protect me. She also didn't make enough money to support the family if my father was gone so I felt that much more obligated to keep what was going on a secret. It was my duty to my sisters to make sure that they were safe and taken care of, and the only person that could do that was our father. If that meant I had to suck it up and allow him to do the things he was doing to me, then that's what I had to do. In some weird, twisted way, that became my one purpose. That was what I was good for. That was my life.

2

"Everybody's having fun

Except me. I'm the lonely one.

I live in shame."

- Ozzy Osbourne, *Goodbye to Romance*

By the time I hit puberty, the abuse had been going on for eight years. Eight years of anything and it just becomes a part of your life, especially when it begins at such a young age. It was all I knew, and I had accepted that was just how it was. There was one problem, though. Growing up a boy means competition, and lots of it. We competed for everything, and when puberty hit, the big competition was about sex. Who was getting it, who was doing what, etc., etc. I have a distinct recollection of standing in the locker room after 8th grade P.E. one day, and somebody was bragging about how they had just gotten their first blow job. I remember thinking, "Oh, big deal. I've been getting them since I was 5". It would have been an instant win according to the laws of male pubescence, but I couldn't tell them that. They wouldn't understand. I had to hide that part of my life. I couldn't be me, even when being me would mean I would "win" at that most important of teenage boy contests. But "me" wasn't socially acceptable. I knew I couldn't tell what was going on and be accepted. Nobody would want to hear about my "accomplishments" in that arena. I knew the things that made me special were the things that I had to hide. They made me a freak and an outcast, and I could never fit in.

Growing up, we weren't a poor family, but we weren't rich, either. We were pretty much middle-class with a mortgage, two cars, and a dog. But with four kids, there wasn't a lot of money to throw around and my clothes showed it. I dressed modestly, never in the latest fashions or anything expensive. Since my parents were buying all of my clothing, it was never what the other kids were wearing and that made me stand out that much more. They were always clean, but never "cool". In fact, somebody wrote in one of my middle school yearbooks "Get some new clothes". I'd like to say it didn't bother me, but it was just one more way for me to feel different.

So I turned to drugs and alcohol. I won't go into every sordid detail about the drugs I did during my teenage years. For one thing, that would fill volumes upon volumes of books. Suffice it to say, not a day went by that I didn't smoke, drink, or ingest some mind-altering substance. I had to. I didn't like myself and being high helped me deal with that fact. Being high gave me an excuse to not be who I really was because, after all, I couldn't be that person. Plus, being high helped me escape into my own head and avoid reality, especially during those times when I was lying naked and helpless, hating my father, hating my life. Being high helped me to "go somewhere else".

But drugs cost money. It was about this time that, instead of beating me, my father would give me cash every time he had sex with me. Looking back, I think to myself, "Why did I allow it to continue if he wasn't beating me any longer?" Years of therapy has led me to realize that, after years and years of beatings and forced sex, I had become conditioned to allow it. It had been part of my life for so long that I just accepted it. Perhaps only the people that have been there will understand that I had no choice.

I didn't want it, but I certainly accepted the cash that went with it. For a 14-year-old boy, that extra $80 or so each week was awesome. I started spending less time at home, and more money on drugs and alcohol. It was mostly pot and LSD, since those were the best buys for the money. At one point, I was buying sheets of LSD (100 doses) for $40 and selling them for $3 each…an easy profit of $260 to supplement the money I was "earning". Despite the fact that I allowed it, it was icky to me, even when I was forced to orgasm. Even though that *did* feel good, I felt betrayed by my own body. I hated the way my body reacted; I hated that something so horrible and unwanted could feel so good; I hated that I had no control over myself. So I did more drugs.

Eventually, I needed something stronger. Marijuana and LSD were good, but they weren't enough. I don't remember how or when I did my first line of meth, but once I did, it was on. Meth made me feel as though I was on top of the world. I *loved* it. I felt as though I had no problems. When I was high on meth, I knew I had my act together and nothing could bother me. There is something magical about meth. If you've never done it, I don't think I could ever explain the way it makes you feel. While pot and LSD were good at helping me escape, meth took that to a whole new level. Of course, meth was *much* more expensive than LSD or marijuana, and that money had to come from somewhere. I found that if I said "No" to certain things, my father would double the money he paid me once I caved and allowed him to do it. He was going to do it anyway, but that little bit of manipulation was the only power I had over the situation so I used it to my advantage. However, that still wasn't enough so I began stealing. I would dig through my mother's pockets and take her cash. I don't know why stealing from her came so easily to me. I guess I believed she owed me. She hadn't done anything to stop the abuse that had now been going on for 11 years or so. She hadn't protected me the way I felt a mother should so I had no problem taking things from her. I also began stealing from where I was working. It wasn't much at first, $20 here and there, but I was quickly becoming a person I never thought I would be.

Meth addiction is a horrible thing. It turns you into a shell of a person. It takes away your empathy, numbs your feelings, wipes out your emotions. I became a robotic version of my old self. Sex, drugs, and money were what my life was about. I had friends, but I chose them not because they were good people, but by how many drugs I could do with and around them. There was nothing as important to me as being high. Not friends, not family, not my future.

Then, one day, it happened. I had just endured another round of unwanted sex with my father, and was heading to my bedroom to be alone when I passed the kitchen and my mother was sitting there. She looked directly at me and said, "You're sick. I know what you're doing back there and you disgust me."

That was all it took. My own mother, who hadn't done a thing to help me all these years, was blaming me for what was happening! The very woman who gave birth to me and should have been protective and loving, was cold, dismissive, and accusatory. If I didn't feel worthless and empty before this, I certainly did now. If I had any shred of empathy or emotion left, this pretty much killed it…except for one thing: No matter how much I hated the world, no matter how tightly I shut myself off and repressed all emotions, no matter how badly I didn't care, deep down inside there was a little boy who just wanted to be loved.

Life wasn't all horrible, though. I took every opportunity to get away from the house and away from my father. That meant going places without him. I had joined the Boy Scouts, but he became the assistant scoutmaster so he was still always around. Thankfully, there were almost always other people around so the opportunity for sex was minimized. The only place I could truly get away was at church retreats.

I had been raised in the church and attended faithfully. I didn't just attend, but actually participated in various ways throughout the years. But as the years went by and I saw how beloved my father was in the congregation, I began to lose interest. After all, even though nobody knew what was going on, I couldn't associate with anybody that would be so enamored with my abuser. It disgusted me. They disgusted me. Over the years, I became more and more disgusted with the hypocrisy of the "church". Often times, there would be potluck lunches after the service, especially around the holidays. Before one particular potluck around Thanksgiving, I slipped out of the service as I frequently did. Sermons bored me and I would take that hour to wander around the Northside area of Berkeley, sometimes crossing campus and visiting Peoples Park. This particular time, I slipped out and went to Telegraph Avenue. I found a homeless person and brought him back to the potluck with me. After all, it was Thanksgiving and he looked like he could use a meal.

You'd have thought I brought a busload of Satan worshipers or strippers with me, judging from the stares and whispers that caused.

I had always believed that doing good, and helping the less fortunate trumped all when it came to practicing our faith. Apparently, that didn't extend to homeless people. He was given a plate of food and a bible, then ushered out the door as quickly and quietly as possible, and nobody ever spoke of it again. That was pretty much the beginning of the end of my belief in the institution of the church. But that didn't stop me from going to the annual summer camps or trips to Mexico.

The camps were a week long, and I *loved* being outdoors and away from my father. Unfortunately, I didn't really fit in. I had long hair, I smoked, I was disgusted with the church as an institution, and I was spending the week with the "normal" church-going kids. They weren't there hiding from an abusive home. They were there to praise the Lord, sing songs, and do Jesus skits and the like. It wasn't as though they actively shunned me, but I wasn't like them, either. I wasn't happy with life. I wore dark clothing, rather than the typical '80's preppy bright colors and turned-up collars that all the popular kids wore. No matter how many years I went, I was never in the "in crowd"; heck, I was barely accepted into the "*out* crowd"! I went every year, but each year I felt more and more like an outcast, more and more removed from what was considered "mainstream". I was becoming alienated. There was a slight benefit to being one of the "bad boys" among all the "good girls" and, looking back, I had some fun times, but I never felt like a part of the group.

I also participated in the annual trips to Mexico, and I loved what we did down there. Not only was it a week away from my father, but our whole reason for going gave me a purpose in life. We would go down and set up tents in a field behind an orphanage in Tijuana, and spend the week donating our time building houses for the poor people that lived in the city dump, building schools, and fixing up the orphanage. It was on one of these trips that I realized that no matter how horrible things were at home, others had it worse. Sure, I had to submit to my father's twisted sexual needs, but at least I had a roof over my head and food to eat. Many of these people barely had that.

One year, one of the family's that we had done some work for invited me into their home at the end of the day, and brought me a plate of food. It was nothing more than tortillas and beans, but the fact that this family had nothing, yet was so grateful for the help they were receiving that they were willing to share what meager food they had was very touching. Yes, there were bugs crawling all over the inside of the bag of tortillas. Yes, the plate was covered in dirt and it looked as though they hadn't washed their hands in weeks before preparing the meal, but I ate it anyway. I ate it because they gave it to me and I wanted to share that moment with them. It was one of the more touching moments of my life.

It was also during one of these Mexico trips that I met a woman who, to this day, I consider the first person I ever really loved. Even though we really only spent one night together, it was magical. We sat on the top of a mound of dirt, looking at the moon, smelling the burning tires that the families in the dump burned for heat, and just talked. I don't remember what we talked about, and I don't remember how long we were there. I just remember feeling that, at last, somebody "got" me. Somebody saw me for me, and I could be honest and open with her.

Unfortunately, she lived in Southern California and I lived in Northern. After the week was up, we went our separate ways and never saw each other again. We kept in touch through letters and phone calls, but those slowed over time. Eventually, I received the dreaded "I care about you, but this is too hard to do at such a distance. Good bye and good luck" letter. I was 17 and that was the first time I ever really felt like I had my heart broken. I remember it was written on pink paper. I remember sitting outside in my friend's back yard, leaning against the clubhouse that we had built, clutching that letter in my hand as the sun beat down on me and my friend was asking me if I was okay.

That was the last time I ever cried, and I swore that I would never let myself get hurt again. This caring thing was too hard. Relationships took too much effort and just ended in pain. Compared to this, my relationship with my father seemed easy.

The church functions and the trips weren't the only time I was able to get out and away from the house, though. I also joined the Boy Scouts at age 11 or 12. I had risen through the ranks of the Cub Scouts, and hopped over to the BSA as soon as I was able. In addition to the weekly meetings where I was safe from my father's advances, we would also go camping at least one weekend every month. It wasn't a clean getaway like the church camps were, though. My father weaseled his way into being the assistant scoutmaster and participated in all the activities. It must have been heaven for him to be around a bunch of pre-pubescent boys, but at least having all of those people around meant I would usually have a weekend free from having to have sex with him. Well, he would find a way from time to time but, in general, it was a lot safer out in the woods than at home. As with the Cub Scouts, I quickly rose through the ranks all the way up from patrol leader, to senior patrol leader, even as far as a junior assistant scoutmaster. By the time I quit, I was three merit badges away from making Eagle Scout. I could have done it, but those three badges were citizenship badges and I really couldn't get behind them.

By the time I was 17, I figured I had been forced to have sex a minimum of 1,500 times, probably closer to 1,800. I had run away and been returned home by the police three times. I had started off as such a good student and now I was failing at school. Nobody seemed to care why that might be happening. Society had failed me. I had no desire to be a "good citizen" and work for those merit badges so I didn't.

But scouting wasn't about the badges anyway, at least not the troop I was in. Like my childhood, I had managed to find a troop that wasn't like the rest. If you wanted to be a by-the-book scout, you didn't join our troop. We were the troublemakers, the misfits, the outcasts. We drank and smoked and cursed and made crude gestures to women driving behind us on our way to campouts. We didn't have uniform inspections, and we made our own rules when it came to earning the merit badges. In fact, we pretty much made our own rules when it came to everything.

Sadly, my father wasn't the only pedophile along for the ride. Somehow I had managed to land myself with the one troop in the area where the scoutmaster would later be arrested and sent to prison for molesting some of the scouts. We all knew it was happening. Why nobody said anything, I'll never know. The scoutmaster would spend unusual amounts of time in one of the boy's tents, and that boy would typically be favored over the rest of us. I didn't care. I was just glad it wasn't happening to me. I had enough to worry about. But, as time went on, it turned out it wasn't just that one boy.

The scoutmaster would frequently have scouts over to his house. He would let us drink and smoke and sit in his hot tub. He would let us watch porn and be crude and loud. He would let us drive his car and shoot his guns. He was a fun guy to be around…until he got you alone. Then he would liquor you up, put on some porn, and start masturbating in front of you and invite you to join in. At least that's what he did with me a few times. I didn't join in and he never pushed it further, but some of the other boys were apparently so taken in by his charisma, which he had a *lot* of, that they went further than I.

This all came out when he moved and, apparently, left behind a photo of a naked boy that the new owners found. They, of course, turned it over to the police and a huge investigation was started. One night, I received a call from the Kensington Police Department and was asked to come into the police station to look at photo after photo after photo to either identify people or explain what was going on. It was a surreal experience. I didn't want to be there. Nothing had happened to me, but they kept pressuring me to identify this kid or that, or explain why so and so had a turkey neck sticking out of his pants, or why everybody was swimming naked. I was there for probably no more than an hour, but it seemed like forever.

Our scoutmaster ended up doing eight years in state prison, and the victims sued him and won in civil court. I don't remember how much money they got and, although I could have joined in the suit, I didn't want to. I was so done with the whole adult/child sex thing that I wanted nothing more to do with any of it. Unfortunately, I was still in high school, and the fact that my father was the assistant scoutmaster made him guilty by association. He was guilty of a lot of things, but I never heard of him touching any of the scouts. But that didn't matter.

One night, I was walking through the park alone and found myself surrounded by 15-20 boys that I went to school with. They all started talking shit about my father and accusing him of all sorts of horrible things related to the investigation, as if it was my fault. I stood my ground for a little while but, deep down, I knew what they were saying was true to some extent. He may not have molested any of the scouts, but he definitely *was* a pedophile. I couldn't deny that. I eventually threw up my hands, saying "Whatever", and left them to their cruel taunts and name calling. As I walked the rest of the way home that night, I knew that I would carry this around with me for the rest of my life. So I went and got stoned and drunk, and pretended that everything was alright.

3

"You're on a suicidal ride of self-destruction

And, in the end, you're gonna crash.

You live too fast."

– Black Sabbath, *Methademic*

I guess you can't say that my teenage years were *all* about drugs and alcohol. I had my music, as well. Growing up, it seemed like there was some unwritten rule in our house that all of us kids had to play some type of musical instrument. I had chosen the saxophone and took lessons for several years, but never really did anything with it. I tried playing in the middle school band, but always played second sax. I never could quite be the best no matter how hard I tried so, in either 7th or 8th grade, I gave it up altogether. I stopped taking lessons and pretty much forgot about the whole thing.

Then, when I was 17 or so, I had a friend who was given a bass guitar, but didn't really want it. He was singing in another band so I convinced him to loan it to me and I started playing. Eventually, his dad made him take it back, but the mother of the drummer I was playing with at the time bought me another bass. We weren't really playing much, just getting stoned, dropping LSD, and playing around, but it got me used to playing with other people. Soon, I had joined up with some other friends to play at the high school talent show. I didn't really like performing in front of people and just stood there throughout the show. I was technically playing everything correctly, but it was all rote mechanical stuff with no feeling. It was fun. It was fast. It was angry, but it wasn't going anywhere.

Eventually, we lost our drummer (our singer was a bit of a tweaker and the drummer didn't feel we were serious enough so he left to go play with people he felt were more serious), and went on the hunt for a new one. We found one, but instead of coming to play with us, he asked if a couple of us wanted to play with the punk band that he was already playing with…Special Forces out of Berkeley, California. They needed a bass player and second guitar so I said yes.

At first, I wasn't sure. After all, here was an established band with two albums, playing dozens of shows per year, with quite a following. I didn't fit in here. They were punk, I had always been a "metalhead". They had shaved heads, I had long hair. But, somehow, we fit. I started practicing with them and was having fun. The music was energetic and angry, and it came easy to me. When it came time for our first show, we shared the bill with a band called Sacrilege, who my friend Gary played with. I had always loved Sacrilege so to be playing a show with them was awesome. Before we went on stage, I drank quite a bit to relax, and relax I did. The show went off without a hitch, and I had fun doing it.

As we left the stage, Gary came over and told me that I had good stage presence, and I took that to heart. After all, I had completely let go up there and let the music flow through me. I was no longer the bass player that just stood there, playing the music, but was bouncing around and actually *feeling* the music. From there on out, every time we took the stage, I went out there and had fun. There was something about playing on stage that made me feel "free". When I was up there, under the lights, I could let go and really be myself. I didn't have any problems. I didn't worry about things or think about anything. My mind was completely clear of anything bad, and those demons that usually haunted me were not just quiet, but seemed to go away. I knew the songs backwards and forwards, and wasn't worried about screwing up or missing some notes. It was all about the energy and freedom for me.

I was a wild, out of control animal on stage and never stopped drinking, even while I was playing. My friend Vince would stand by my amp and pour beer down my throat in the middle of songs just so I could keep drinking without stopping. One night, while playing one of our largest shows with The Mentors and Verbal Abuse, I jumped off the drum riser and my aim was off. I hit my bass cabinet and flipped over backwards, falling off the back of the stage, but I never missed a beat. As always, Vince was there to help pick me up so I wouldn't have to stop playing. Other times, I would jump off the stage into the pit with my bass, but I managed to never hit anybody. Falling over was just a by-product of the energy, I suppose.

It wasn't long before we were heading out on tour. We had shows lined up all along the West Coast, and a truck to ride in, so we were set. My parents were dead set against it. They didn't seem to appreciate that I had found something that I really enjoyed doing and made me happy. Since I was still living at home, they tried to tell me I couldn't go. When I told them there was no way I was going to miss out on this opportunity, I was informed that if I chose to go, I would not have a place to live when I returned. I was okay with that. I knew I had the option of moving in with my girlfriend, Sandie, and it would get me away from my father.

So I went.

And it was awesome.

It was a small tour. Los Angeles, Fresno, Berkeley, Sacramento, Eugene, Portland, Walla Walla, and Tacoma. We were supposed to follow that up with a show in Seattle and then into Canada, heading East with the DayGlo Abortions, but we never made it. I'm not sure why we cancelled Seattle, but I seem to recall we wouldn't be able to get into Canada. That didn't matter at the time. The adventure we did have was incredible. The shows were awesome and, since we were from out of town, we were treated well. People would give us food, let us crash at their place, give us booze and drugs. We gave a live radio interview in Eugene, Oregon, and when we left, there was a small crowd of people in the parking lot waiting to party with us. It was quite the experience having people that just wanted to be around us because we played in a band.

But, even then, I didn't feel as though I fit in. I talked the talk and walked the walk, but I never really felt as though I was accepted. I even felt distant with my own band mates. Many years later, I ran into the guitarist in a bar and told him that I always felt that he didn't like me. He was shocked and told me that he had considered quitting the band several times, but he stayed because he really enjoyed playing with me.

I had spent so many years being "different" and carrying around the secret that made me withdrawn and insecure that I couldn't be comfortable and relaxed around other people, even when I had no reason not to be. I had so many years of believing that I was only good for sex and that I had nothing else to offer people that I had begun to approach every relationship that way. I frequently felt as though my body was there, but I was actually standing outside of myself, keeping myself safe, keeping away from people because to allow them to know the real me was to let myself get hurt. I had just spent the last 80% of my life prostituting myself to my father, and I was finally free of that. I wasn't about to allow myself to get hurt again. Unfortunately, that also meant I wasn't able to allow myself to truly experience all that life was offering. So what was supposed to be one of the most awesome times of my life was marred by the fact that I really had no idea how to be me. Not only did I have no idea how to be me, I didn't *want* to be me.

Over the next couple of years, we played dozens upon dozens of live shows, did live radio, even got to be the band on stage during a Hollywood movie bar scene. People loved to party with us. We always had people hanging around, I had groupies... well, ok... I could have had *lots* of groupies. There was certainly no shortage of women that I could have been having sex with, but that wasn't my thing for two reasons. Number one – I had just spent the previous 13 years having all that unwanted sex with my father. Sex, to me, wasn't anything wonderful or exciting. In my mind, sex = love = pain, and I didn't want that.

Number two, I had a girlfriend at the time. For whatever reason, I felt a connection with Sandie that I didn't feel with any of these other women. She seemed to actually like me for who I was and not who I could be when I was drinking or high. Plus, she let me move in with her at her mom's house. With the exception of that one night in Mexico, it was the first time I had really felt accepted by anybody that wasn't just out to have sex with me. I don't know at what point I told her about my father, or how much I ever did manage to tell her, but she didn't hold it against me. I felt comfortable with her to the point where we got a place and moved in together.

We had met at a mutual friend's house where we would smoke pot and do cocaine. He would typically only host small gatherings, maybe 6-8 people at the most, so we had the opportunity to really connect. Sandie was beautiful. She had a great body and, most importantly, she was a free spirit who did things her own way. I loved that about her, and when she gave me a ride home one night, I "accidentally" left my skateboard in her car so I would have an excuse to see her again. There was something about her that I felt drawn towards, and I felt free when I was around her. Free to talk, free to laugh, free to be the best me I knew how to be. I don't doubt that she had her own demons, but that didn't matter. In fact, I suspect it made it easier for us to connect on a deeper level. Of course, with my history, that deeper level was a mixed blessing.

During my time with the band, I had gotten more and more into meth, and it had become a controlling part of my life. I had spent so much of my life not knowing who I was that I let the meth control everything, and it completely took over my life. I was so focused on getting more of it and being high that all common sense went out the window. I stole from my girlfriend's mom, I lied to the people who cared about me and at one point, when I was out picking up some meth for a couple of friends, I even found myself face down, cuffed, a gun pointed at the back of my head while the DEA went through my pockets.

You might think that would be enough to stop, but that just shows that you were never a meth addict.

Eventually, I was kicked out of the band because I had become unreliable, but I was okay with that. I felt they never liked me anyway so what did I care. I had a job that I was quickly rising through the ranks at, I had proposed to my girlfriend and she had accepted, we had our own place. What more did I need? I didn't need my past any longer. It was full of pain and anger and loneliness. I had everything right in front of me and was poised to have a great life.

If only it worked that way.

I struggled with the meth addiction for years. Sandie was patient and put up with it, but she never really knew the extent of how much I was doing. I had spent my whole life hiding deep, dark secrets from people, and this was no different. I had been doing it for so long that I was able to be high all day, then sleep at night. I was able to eat and do all the things a non-user would do so there were really few clues. Sure there were times, sometimes months, when I would quit, but since I had never worked on my childhood issues, I was always just one thought away from going right back into it.

I did try really hard to become a different person. I had received a couple of promotions at work and was handling medical malpractice claims, which I actually enjoyed doing. I was working for the insurance company, though, so my job was to either get rid of the cases or settle them for as little as possible. I was working with the yuppie crowd, which was a far cry from the punk crowd I had just left. I wore a tie to work, I dressed in yuppie clothes, I was making more money than I ever had before. I had it made.

But I still didn't feel like I fit in, and even less so than with the punks. I had just spent all those years hating people who had it better than me. Not that it was their fault, but I was always jealous of my friends who had it good and seemed happy. And now, here I was, surrounded by grown-up versions of them. I wanted to fit in and be one of them, but I didn't. I couldn't.

Eventually, this ongoing battle in my head became too much. I didn't know how to really be anybody. All I knew was that I still felt empty inside, and no matter how much I surrounded myself with people I wanted to be like, no matter how much I tried to have a good relationship with my wife, no matter how much I tried to become a "grown up", I could never fill that emptiness. I could be surrounded by a dozen people and still be lonely inside. Sure, I was able to fake it. It wasn't as though I sat in a corner by myself and ignored everybody, but I was pretty dead inside.

But I did learn one thing through all of this. I learned how people wanted me to act. I became really good at hiding my true self and only showing people what I knew they wanted to see. So, naturally, people liked me. And when they liked me, I could get them to do things for me. Over the years, I became a master manipulator. I learned how to read people and used that to my advantage to allow me to continue on doing my drugs and getting the things I needed, such as money for more drugs. Since I really didn't care about them, I had no problem using them. I was out for myself and didn't care what damage lay in my wake.

But I wasn't the horrible person that I had become, either. I didn't *want* to be somebody who didn't care. I didn't *want* to hurt people. But I didn't know any other way. It was all about survival, and this is how my brain had been trained to behave. Deep down, I wanted to be liked for me. That little boy inside me still just wanted to find somebody to love him and keep him safe, but that little boy wasn't allowed out. The world was mean and horrible, and people couldn't be trusted. Those that did care were undoubtedly going to hurt him and I couldn't allow that so I locked him in the basement of my soul, built a wall around him, and shut out the light. From time to time, I would hear him crying out, but I was able to ignore him and he would go away. The world was no place for him. He had emotions, he felt things, he was weak.

It probably should go without saying, but my marriage didn't last long. It's hard to be in a relationship when you can't even be yourself, but that wasn't because of her. Sure, I could easily find ways to blame her. I was able to convince myself that she was controlling, she was self-absorbed, she was a bitch. But the real problem with our relationship wasn't with her. I'm sure she had her issues...after all, she was with me…but I wasn't exactly the best husband. The closer we grew, the more distant I became. I began really withdrawing into myself and stopped talking to her. The more distant I became, the more confused and scared I got, which manifested in always being angry with her. I didn't want to lose her. She was the first person that had accepted me for me for any length of time, but I couldn't keep her, either. Again, I was back to that whole issue with caring = hurt that I had been taught so well from childhood.

And it wasn't as though I could just "change my mind" and start thinking differently. When children experience trauma at a young age, their brains develop neural pathways that help them cope with that trauma. There are two things that help people overcome and deal with trauma in a healthy way…the ability to control the outcome, and the ability to make sense of what happened. As a five-year-old, I neither had any control over what my father was doing, nor did I have any idea what it was all about. Five-year-olds don't know about sex.

So I had no coping skills available to me for processing the trauma that I was living with growing up. As a result, my brain and nervous system had wired itself differently from those children who weren't living with repeated traumas. I had been "hard-wired" into protective mode. I had to live inside my own head in order to survive. I had to not trust the people closest to me.

So no matter how badly I wanted it, there was no way that my marriage was going to last. I tried my best, but the harder I tried and the closer we grew, the more I needed to run away in my head, which I did. Quite successfully, I might add.

After spending a couple of years trying and trying to overcome the misfires in my brain, I seemed to give up and just said "Screw it". Sandie and I separated, and I cut loose. It was as if I had been building up for the past two years, and it all needed to escape. I was in my early 20's, had a good job, was living in my grandparent's house up in the hills. My grandfather had died and my grandmother couldn't live alone so Sandie and I had convinced my mom to let us stay there while we helped fix up the place. Of course, once we separated and she moved out, that "fixing up" turned into anything but. It was a huge house, more than 3,300 square feet of living space with a huge living room, formal dining room, and library. It had three stories with three bedrooms upstairs and a very cool wood-paneled room with a wet bar in the basement. There was a small balcony off the living and dining rooms that looked out over a large terraced backyard with a pond and several large trees, with the San Francisco Bay and Golden Gate Bridge in the distance. It was the perfect place for parties. At this point, it seemed like everything was going right for me. I had driven the friend of a friend on a speed run one night and he took me into his dealer's house. We walked into his room and I was shocked. There was an old friend that I hadn't seen in years! As it turned out, he was losing his place to live and I had a TON of room where I was so, within the month, he had moved in.

As a meth addict, having a drug dealer living in my house and paying his rent in meth was *heaven*. The downhill slide for me was quick and easy, but I didn't see it as bad. It didn't last long, but it was definitely intense. We didn't eat much and I sometimes wonder how the hell we managed to survive, especially considering a good 90% of my income was spent on booze and meth. We had the most incredible parties that would start on Thursdays and not end until Tuesday, sometimes not even then. People would come from all over the area to party at "the green house in the hills", and having cops at my door wasn't unusual. There was one time that I arrived home from work, walked into my living room, and there had to be at least 75 people there...and I didn't know a single one of them! That didn't last very long, though, after one of them tried to kick me out, saying I didn't belong at *their* party. Heck, I didn't belong anywhere. Why should I belong in my own house? But, we got rid of them and after that, we typically kept it to a more intimate 50-100 people. I met some great people that came through there, people I am friends with to this day, but, for the most part, it was a blur. I would go to my car in the mornings and find beer cans stacked on it by the neighbors who didn't seem to appreciate beer cans and bottles left in their yards. I would go to the store and everybody would know me as "that guy". I even had a friend, who was lost and looking for directions, actually get directions from a police officer once he told him where he was trying to go. It was a wild and crazy time.

But despite the hundreds of people that wandered through there, I was always lonely. I didn't feel like being in any sort of relationship after having my marriage fail, which I took very personally – but for all the wrong reasons. Even though, as the "owner" of the big party house, I had many opportunities to have various sexual encounters with random women, I just wasn't into it. For one thing, I was too shy. I don't think anybody who knew me would ever describe me as that, but it was true. I actually had naked women crawl into my bed with me and I ignored them. Sex was great, it felt good, but it wasn't something that was all that important to me. In fact, I almost didn't enjoy it thanks to how I had grown up, and it certainly wasn't something that I went out of my way for. I was still in that mode of trying to escape my childhood in any way possible.

I'm not sure how my second wife and I managed to start seeing each other, but it was there at the "party house" that we met for the first time…

4

"Happiness I cannot feel, and love to me is so unreal."

– Black Sabbath, *Paranoid*

Mentally and emotionally, I was in a tough spot. I was doing great at work. They really liked me there, but they didn't know the real me. The real me was only good for having sex with and I knew that wouldn't get me very far in my job so I had to pretend to be somebody else. I was also in my early 20s, had two cars, lots of friends, a good job, and a roof over my head. I guess one might think that I had my act together. But that was on the outside. The inside was a different story. Children need to bond with their parents. They need to feel special. They need to know they are safe. And, most importantly, they need to know they are loved. The amazing thing about the brain is that it can, and will, adapt in whatever way it feels is best. But the coping skills we develop as abused children frequently don't help us in adulthood. In fact, they can seriously hinder our lives later on.

It wasn't as though I didn't feel loved. I knew my father loved me, even though he showed it in such wrong ways. I was close with my sisters, especially my older sister. When we were really young, my mother, before she started drinking a lot, was always there. She would take us on trips to the grocery store where they had a playroom for the kids while the parents shopped. She would take us to the movies, or give us rides wherever we needed to go. She encouraged us to play our music and take up a sport. But she could also be very hands-off. She wanted us to learn our lessons through natural consequences so she allowed us to fail, although it wasn't uncommon to hear "I told you so" from her. She wasn't a warm person. She meant well, I believe, but she wasn't a hugging/touching kind of person. I don't recall her saying "I love you" much. Those were the kinds of things I had to turn to my father for. Our parents created a physically safe world for us, but it was emotionally cold where our mother was concerned. I can't speak for my sisters' relationship with our father, but he was the warm, touchy, hugging parent for me. However, given all that was going on, those touches and hugs never really felt safe.

I was still in the "need to be loved" / "scared to be loved" mindset. The little boy inside me was crying out for somebody to show that they cared about him, while my grown-up self kept telling him to shut up because he didn't know what he was asking for. I had come up with all sorts of justifications as to why my marriage hadn't worked out, and I was dead set against anything like that happening again.

I'm not sure how I met Pam, other than it was at a party at my house. She was everything I was looking for. Not just because of the fact that she was tall and exotic looking, but she was confident, strong, seemed to have her act together, and she didn't throw herself at me like some of the other women had done. Looking back, I suspect what really attracted me to her was the fact that she was emotionally aloof, highly independent, and damaged. She wanted me because I had a job, a car, a home. I wanted her because she didn't seem to want to get too close and I "needed" somebody. It was a perfect match.

It was not surprising that she was also a meth addict.

When the days of the "party house" drew to a close, she and I moved into a room at her friend's house, although he was more of her dealer than her friend. We weren't the only people to be crashing there. Every time I would get up and head downstairs to go to work, there would be at least a half dozen tweakers sitting around in the living room, wondering who the hell this guy in the suit was. I never really talked to them. In fact, I rarely even spoke to the guy whose house we were living in. I was focused on my job and being with Pam. I had been living with stress all my life, and there were times that I just couldn't handle anymore. I was always on the verge of total overload. At this point in time, I just couldn't handle any additional stimulation, and that included meeting new people. As outgoing and energetic as meth tends to make people, I had somehow found a way to retreat into my own shell. I was living in a tunnel. At one end was my work, and at the other end was the one room I stayed in. I didn't really stray too far outside of those two locations.

Over the next six months, I did meet some people at that house. After all, we did all live together, although it wasn't until the water and electricity got shut off that I found out we weren't supposed to be there at all. I still pretty much kept to myself, focused on work and meth. Getting emotionally involved with anybody, even on just a friendship level, was too much work and not something that I was going to allow to happen. A few of them seemed like decent people, but I didn't trust any of them. They were all meth addicts. Of course, I didn't realize at the time that the only real difference between me and them was that I had a job. Other than that, we were all in the same boat. But I couldn't see that because I didn't want it to be true. I was better than that. I wasn't some loser meth addict. I was Steve. I had survived and I had my act together. I knew that, any day now, everything would fall into place.

I had no idea what that would look like. I still had no dreams or plans for my future, but I knew that everything was going to work out if I just stuck it out long enough.

When we all got kicked out of that house, Pam and I moved into a nearby motel. It was in a slightly better part of town than we had been living in, and the rates were affordable. I knew it was only temporary since I was looking for a place of our own, but it had all the amenities I needed – a toilet, a shower, and a liquor store next door.

Over the next month or so, I got to know all the homeless people that hung out downstairs and in front of the liquor store. I was only three blocks from where my former guitar player lived, but I never visited him. I was too ashamed of how far I had fallen. I still had my job and all my teeth, but this definitely wasn't how I deserved to live. It wasn't the life I wanted my family to have. Pam had a daughter from a previous relationship who was living with her grandfather (dad was in prison and mom obviously couldn't take care of her), and I wanted the three of us to be together. I had always liked little kids and this girl was pretty awesome so, with her in mind, I went out and found an apartment.

It wasn't big. I could only afford a one bedroom and I was supposed to be living there alone, according to the landlord, but I brought Pam in anyway. We finally had a place of our own. We could soon live as a family (being a one bedroom, it meant that we couldn't yet have her daughter there, but soon!). Things were falling into place like I always knew they would.

Except for one thing…we were both still hooked on meth. That really was the focal point of our lives. We were okay as long as we had it, and when we were out, all we cared about was getting more. With me now paying rent and her not working at all, I didn't have as much money left over to buy it. She had her beautician's license, but wasn't doing anything with it. She believed working was beneath her, and if she *was* going to work, she certainly wasn't going to work for minimum wage. So she didn't work at all.

Which meant that our money didn't go far. Between gas, food, and meth, we were always tight. In fact, we never really had enough money to support our habit so she would always head over to her dealer's house, alone, and somehow come back with a bag. I kind of suspected that she was performing sexual favors in exchange, but didn't want to rock the boat. I would never say I was "happy" with where I was in life at that point in time, but the known is always less scary than the unknown, and I didn't have the emotional and mental strength to make changes in my life right then. I was barely holding it together as it was.

Besides, I needed the meth. It helped keep my own demons at bay. It helped me believe that everything was okay, that things really weren't as bad as they seemed. Yes, she was cold and heartless when she was high. Yes, I had to leave work every afternoon to pick up her daughter from school because she would be sleeping and always forget to do it. But, hey, I had a good life, right?

So we got married.

I look back now and wonder what the hell I was thinking. I was in such a bad spot in my life mentally, emotionally, and physically (I would get out of breath just brushing my teeth) that I don't know what I was thinking. Here was this woman that treated me like crap, who didn't take care of her daughter, who was whoring herself out for drugs, and I was willing to overlook all of that for the sake of not turning my life upside down yet again. My life had been so full of bad, I had been physically and mentally abused for so long, that it was normal. Much like how you can tie an elephant to a small wooden stake and he won't run away since he has been conditioned to believe that once he's tied up, it's useless to try. I had been conditioned to believe that this was how life was. My father was still trying to get me to come have sex with him for money, my wife was still sleeping around for drugs, and this all seemed perfectly normal to me.

Besides, when she was sleeping, she would tell me she loved me so I knew it had to be true. And since love meant allowing others to treat you like crap, I really had it all. That little boy in me could have his love, and the adult in me could feel vindicated that he was right – love was painful and horrible and wonderful all at the same time.

By this time, I had alienated pretty much all of my friends. They were good people, but they couldn't really do anything for me. I was still constantly on the edge of a total breakdown so I had to focus my limited mental energy on things that could keep propelling me forward. My step-daughter still wasn't living with us so I found a two bedroom place and we moved. I thought this would be the change that would make everything all better, but the rent was higher and my wife still refused to work so we had even less money. I was hitting the food banks to make it through in between paychecks. I was slipping out of work early to pick up and deliver my daughter home. I was barely keeping it together.

To top it off, I kept getting into trouble with the law. It was small things – driving a car with expired registration, driving on a suspended license, missing my court dates. Victimless crimes, for sure, but they started to catch up to me. The first time I was arrested and taken out to the county jail, my work overlooked it. It was only for a few days, and I guess I had some sick days saved up so they applied those and pretended nothing happened. But when it happened again, and then again, they let me go.

Fired!

I had always seemed to have a job. From the time I was 14-years-old, I was working, and these weren't babysitter-type jobs, although I also did those from time to time. I started off teaching swim classes to really young kids. That was fun and I enjoyed it. From there, I went on to get my lifeguarding certificate and started spending more time out of the water than in it. I did this all through high school and really loved it. I don't know if I loved it for the fact that it gave me purpose, it gave me money, or that it got me out of the house, but that doesn't matter. Working became a part of who I was, and I have taken that with me throughout my adulthood. I delivered pizzas, I served up frozen yogurt, I worked the graveyard shift at a gas station, I even drove a truck and cleaned out portable toilets for a while. I loved to work. It gave me a feeling of accomplishment. It got me away from the horror in which I was living at home. It was a place of safety.

I had been fired before, but never without having something to fall back on. This time was different. I was a meth addict, I had a criminal record, I had no real skills. I *had* spent some time in college, earning a whopping 28 units, although about 1/3 of those were core classes, 1/3 were electives such as Medical Terminology, and the rest were "weight training" since it was cheaper than joining a gym. There really wasn't much education there to speak of that would help me find a job.

I had a wife and daughter I needed to take care of, and I couldn't find a job. If I thought I was stressed out before, this made that seem like a piece of cake.

Thankfully, losing my job didn't mean that my wife lost her connection so we still had the meth to keep us going. By this time, I was completely lost. I started hanging out with another meth addict down the street. I knew him from the nightclub I used to hang out at. He had sung for a band that I loved, until he was shot and paralyzed from the waist down. He had his issues and I had mine so we hung out together and did our dope. It didn't last long, but it was very much reminiscent of my "party house". It was familiar and, therefore, comfortable.

But as interesting as it was there, there wasn't an unending supply of free dope so I moved on. I needed to find work and was sending out resumes as fast as I could, but nobody was biting.

To really add to the chaos that had become my life, during the investigation of my former scoutmaster's pedophilic activities, it came out that my father had also molested one of my sisters. Once my mother found out about that, she kicked him out of the house that they had just rebuilt. I wasn't sure how to feel about that. I remember being so angry that he would do that to my sister. How dare he?! I felt like all those years of submitting to him and trying to keep him away from my sisters was useless. I had let myself be used and for what? I began to dislike myself even more, and the realization that the one person I thought really loved me had done this to one of my sisters was crushing. He didn't care about me, he didn't care about anybody. That much was obvious now. Plus, the fact that my mother jumped up and instantly defend her against him, throwing him out in the cold as soon as she found out, was awesome. But why hadn't she done that for me? She knew. I know she knew because she said so. So why wasn't I worth defending? She obviously had it in her to defend her children, just not me.

I wasn't worth it.

I guess I wasn't all that shocked, really. I had always felt distant from my mother. I'm glad she defended my sister. The fact that she didn't defend me didn't matter. I easily slipped into a world of "whatever". I convinced myself that I didn't care. I had other things to worry about. Specifically, how was I going to provide for my family? I answered an ad for a firefighting job and it turned out to be a US Navy recruiting office. I had talked to Navy recruiters before. At the end of high school, I took the ASVAB test and scored in the 98th percentile. But I wasn't military material back then. I just wanted to do my drugs and play my music. This time around was different, though. I was desperate. Besides, a friend of mine (a former meth dealer) had gone into the Navy and it seemed to do him some good.

So I went and talked to the recruiters, then signed the papers.

Boot camp was still months away, and I needed to pay the rent until then. It wasn't as if I got some huge bonus for signing up. So I kept looking for a job and finally found one at a department store. The holidays were coming up and a lot of places were hiring seasonal workers. The fact that I was going into the Navy on Feb 1st seemed to impress them so they hired me and put me in the "pickup" department. I worked the counter and would assist with people's packages when they came to pick them up. It was simple, it was brainless, it was a job.

But it didn't pay well. It paid better than not having a job at all, but I needed more money. So I started grabbing $20 here, $50 there. It didn't take long for store security to figure out what was going on. Then one night, when I was really desperate and needed to pay my rent, I took $200 and set it aside. Something told me not to take it so I stashed it under a box in the warehouse and went home. The next day, I arrived at work and security grabbed me, took me into the back, and started asking me about the money. I told them were to find it and they got it back. They called the police who arrested me and held me in the county jail for three days, but since the money wasn't technically missing, they didn't charge me with anything and released me.

I think it doesn't need to be said that I lost that job.

But that was okay. I was leaving for boot camp in about two weeks. As my departure time grew closer, I called the District Attorney's office and talked to them about what had happened. I told them I was leaving for boot camp and wanted to make sure there was nothing hanging over me. They assured me that there was no case, that no charges would be filed, and that I was free to leave.

I would find out years later that wasn't exactly true.

5

"He hides himself away. His secrets not revealed.

As life just passes by, he keeps himself concealed."

– Black Sabbath, *Loner*

Boot camp was quite the experience. It wasn't bad. In fact, I almost enjoyed it. The longest I had been sober up to that point was ten days, but that's while I was in jail once. That was nothing like this. I didn't have time for withdrawals. Between the incredible amount of exercising and the studying, there wasn't time for much. I missed my wife and step-daughter, but I knew that this would only last two months, and I could do anything for two months.

So I dove into it with gusto, and got myself into the best shape I had ever been in. Most of the people who knew me before I went in would probably be shocked to hear that I actually did really well. I did well enough that I was one of the top three recruits in my company and was given the opportunity to go to advanced training. So when they asked me to choose ten rates (jobs) that I wanted to study and do while in the Navy, I chose all the ones that I thought sounded fun and/or would help me prepare for a future. It was mostly things having to do with planes, electronics, and weapons. But the one thing I *really* wanted to do was underwater ordinance. I thought blowing stuff up would be fun, and since I had been a swim instructor and lifeguard, the water thing was right up my alley.

So I submitted my list of the ten things I really wanted to do, and I sat back and waited. After a week or so, I heard that they had selected what school they were going to send me to after boot camp. I was excited. In fact, this was one of the most exciting things in my life. I had really pulled it all together and now I was going to either blow stuff up, or learn a skill that would carry me through the rest of my life. Either way, I couldn't lose.

That is until I opened the envelope. What they had selected for me had nothing to do with planes or electronics, and it couldn't have been further from blowing stuff up. Rather, they had decided to send me to Meridian, Mississippi, to train as a Personnelman. Seriously?? All that hoopla and they were just going to have me do paperwork? I was going to handle people's service records? Talk about a disappointment.

But whatever. It felt great to be in really good physical shape and off the drugs. It didn't really matter where they were going to send me. The important thing was that I was taking back control, even though I really wasn't. After all, every minute of every day was planned out. Whether it was school or exercise or church, which everybody had to attend, there wasn't really any "me" time, except for Sunday afternoons. So I didn't really have much time to slow down and think about things. I was so busy that I didn't have time to realize how lonely I was. I was 27, most of the people in my company were 18 or 19; I had a step-daughter, they were still kids themselves. I didn't have much in common with them so, yet again, I was the outsider.

Boot camp graduation was on April 1st. My wife, step-daughter, and father-in-law all came out for the graduation. My dad was in prison at the time so I knew he wouldn't be there. My mother didn't come, either. I don't remember why, but I don't think I really cared at that point. I was so happy to be done with my family and moving on to a better life, even if I was just going to be doing stupid paperwork for the next 2.5 years. But I had survived boot camp, and was soon on a plane heading to Mississippi for eight weeks of training. Once I arrived there, I was able to fly my wife and step-daughter out so we could all stay in the family housing.

Because I had my family there, I didn't stay in the dorms like 98% of my classmates so I missed out on all that bonding and pretty much stayed to myself. But since I wasn't in the dorms, I wasn't subject to their "No Alcohol" rule so I always had my beer with me. But I didn't drink too much. After all, crawling out of bed with a hangover and having to go exercise and run for an hour is never much fun. So, somehow, I managed to keep my drinking to a respectable amount. School finally ended, with me near the top of my class again. As with the middle school band, I never managed to make it to number one, but I was close. I had gotten my orders and was set to fly out to meet my ship, the USS Puget Sound (AD38), which was leaving soon for a six month cruise in the Mediterranean Sea.

So we all flew back to California for about a week, then I was gone again. After a two day stopover in Sicily, I met up with my ship in Xania, Crete. I had been assigned to a repair ship, whose job was primarily in port. We didn't stay out at sea for more than a few days at a time during the entire cruise, with the exception of crossing the Atlantic Ocean on our way back home. So with my work schedule being on duty every 3rd day, that gave us two days at a time to explore. We had regular work hours, but once 5pm rolled around, everybody headed to the liberty boats to head ashore.

Portugal, Spain, Italy, France, Greece, Turkey, as well as the islands of Mallorca, Sicily, and Crete were our stops.

And I got drunk at every one. We've all heard the stories about how much sailors drink when they go ashore, and I lived up to every one of those stories. I was free for the first time in my life – no wife/girlfriend to really worry about. She rarely answered the phone when I called home since she was always out with her friends doing whatever she was doing. I had no kids to be responsible for, no father trying to have sex with me, no drug habit to control me. It was as if I had been set free from all the things that had held me back over the years. Yes, I had to work (it *is* a job, after all), but that didn't bother me. I had been working solid for the past 13 years. I was used to it and it was part of who I was.

So I cut loose. Whether it was running through the alleys in Greece because somebody I was with had just shattered a huge window at the bar and we were trying to get him to safety; hanging out with some guy who called himself "El Al Capone de Palma" who sold pot from under the seat of his moped until the cops came and made us go back to the ship; or being stuck on shore and having to sleep in a castle courtyard in France, being given cots for the night by the French Air Force, then free pastries and coffee in the morning by the locals, every day was an adventure.

And I was drunk through it all.

Somebody had a copy of Pink Floyd's *The Wall,* and I watched that movie over and over on those nights that I couldn't leave the ship. I could totally relate to the main character and how alone he felt. How he was surrounded by all these people, yet he was a scared, lonely little boy inside. So I would just sit there and watch the movie, over and over, waiting for the cruise to end so I could go home because, deep down, I was really lonely and wanted to be home where things were familiar. I was having the time of my life but, despite the dysfunctional family life I had at home, I felt drawn to it. I missed it. I needed it.

When we did finally arrive home in Virginia, I took leave and went home to California to grab my wife and step-daughter. During the entire cruise, I had remained faithful to my marriage. Many of my shipmates talked about the "Navy marriage", which meant that you were free to sleep around once you were more than 20 miles offshore, but that wasn't my thing. It wasn't as if I didn't have the opportunity. I just didn't care to. Sex still wasn't something I pursued like most of the guys I knew. Besides, I was probably far too drunk most of the time that I was overseas. Drinking was the only way I knew to deal with the loneliness.

So my oldest daughter was conceived the night I arrived home. She is, and will always be, my "welcome home" baby.

We all moved out to Virginia, where I would work on the ship, and my wife would isolate herself. She had no drugs out there, and no way to get them. I was drinking a lot, and really have little recollection of how things went. Being a parent was still new to me and, given the role models I had growing up, I'm actually surprised that I managed to somewhat pull it off. As my wife's pregnancy progressed, her mother became more and more sick. She had been diagnosed with breast cancer, and my wife wanted to go back and be with her. She went back a couple of times over the course of the year, but the stress was becoming more and more. At one point, I had petitioned the Navy to transfer me back to California because my wife had been ordered to bed rest due to the stress, and she was there with her dying mother and our young daughter. But they refused, and I had to remain in Virginia while my seven-year-old step-daughter took care of my bed-ridden pregnant wife and her dying grandmother. I felt powerless and was pretty angry at the Navy for not helping me.

But they came back to Virginia for my daughter's birth. It was a proud day for me, but it didn't last. Eleven days later, my mother-in-law died and my family moved back to California for good. I only had about six months left in the Navy so they were going to set up in California and I would join them when I got out.

It was the longest six months of my life. I was so incredibly lonely that I began drinking more and more. I spent all of my money on booze, and my electricity ended up being shut off for non-payment. I was behind in my rent. I wasn't doing drugs, but I was an empty shell of a person, and the only way I knew to fill that void was to drown it in alcohol. All of the things that had kept my mind off what had happened to me as a child were gone. I had nothing to distract me and my PTSD began kicking in full force. So I drank. And drank. And drank.

One night at the bar… well, it was actually a strip club. Seeing as how I had spent my late teens / early 20s around strippers, porn stars, and rock star types, I don't think it's too surprising that's where I gravitated to again, and I had made good friends with the strippers there. That night, I was standing out front, after drinking a good amount of tequila, and some guy I had been talking to inside was leaving. We had been talking about his upcoming wedding and I'm not sure what I said but, the next thing I knew, he was holding a knife to my throat, telling me he was going to kill me.

I don't know what he expected, but I didn't care if I lived or died so I began talking back to him. I said things like "What kind of man pulls a weapon on an unarmed person? I'd rather die like a man than be a pussy like you", and pushing into the knife and daring him to go ahead and do it. Finally, he put down the knife. I took off my jacket, getting ready to fight, but he jumped into his car and took off. Not being willing to accept that, I hopped in my car and chased him down, then proceeded to beat the crap out of him until somebody pulled me off of him. I was in such a frenzy that I didn't realize it was a police officer pulling me off so I threatened to stick toothpicks in his eyes if he didn't let go.

That earned me a nice little 72-hour hold in the psych ward at the Navy hospital.

Thankfully, all my years of manipulating people paid off, and I was able to convince them that it was a one-time, alcohol-fueled mistake so they let me go.

As my discharge date got closer, I ramped up the drinking. My daughter was back in California with my wife, who was back on the meth big time. She and her brother were fighting it out over the house and property, and my daughter wasn't safe, but there was nothing I could do. The Navy wouldn't let me go early so I kept drinking.

Of course, the more I drank, the lonelier I became. It was ironic that I drank to fill the hole in my soul, but the drinking was only making that hole larger. One night, I couldn't take it any longer. I was living in an apartment with no electricity. I can't remember the last time I had eaten anything away from the ship, and I had spent all of my money at the bar, drinking and playing pool. Thoughts of my childhood surfaced and I was angry. Really angry. Angry at my father for raping me, angry at my mother for not caring, angry at the world. I couldn't take it anymore.

So I picked up the phone and called 911. When they answered, I told them that I needed help. That I was going to hurt somebody. That I might hurt myself.

So I got another 72-hour hold in the Navy psych hospital.

Of course, as soon as I got there, I wanted to leave. I really just needed to know that SOMEBODY out there cared. That somebody out there actually cared enough to make sure I was okay. I pretty much got that as soon as I arrived at the hospital so I was done with it and ready to leave. They wouldn't let me leave at first, but I finally managed to convince them that I was okay, that it wouldn't happen again, and that they couldn't keep me there without a court order anyway.

So, after three days, I left.

I didn't have a car so one of my shipmates sold me his. Well, I wouldn't say "sold". I was simply supposed to take over the payments while I drove it.

But I didn't pay. I definitely drove it, but when the registration expired, I didn't bother to renew. After all, it wasn't my car and I was back in that state of mind where I could only think about myself. I was always on the edge of a total breakdown, and couldn't handle the responsibility of something even as simple as being a decent person so I did whatever I wanted and didn't care about the outcome…until the police pulled me over for a bad registration.

I had been drinking, but I wasn't drunk. I might have even gotten away with it if it hadn't been for one thing – the wife and I had taken a "staycation" in a local hotel about six months prior. I had written two checks – one for the room, and one for something else. Those checks had bounced but, apparently, my wife had hidden those notices because I was totally unaware of any of it.

So I was taken in on a felony warrant. I spent a few days in jail before some organization posted my bail for me. I wasn't sure who they were, only that they assisted with bail for service members. I guess they figured it was safe since we weren't going anywhere.

Boy, were they wrong. My flight home from the Navy on my discharge date was scheduled for an hour after my court appearance. I couldn't do both. So I did the obvious thing. I skipped court and hopped on the plane back to California.

What I returned to was far worse than just me now being a felon on the run…

6

"Don't you think I know what I'm doing?

Don't tell me that it's doing me wrong.

You're the one who's really a loser.

This is where I feel I belong"

– Black Sabbath, *Snowblind*

If there was any mental health counselling available in the Navy other than in the psycho ward, I wasn't aware of it. I probably wouldn't have taken advantage of it anyway. After all, I knew what had happened to me. I had processed it, and it didn't bother me. What was done was done, right? I had a daughter to raise, I needed to find a job, and I was fresh out of the military. The world was wide open.

It didn't take me long to find a job. Being able to put recent military service on my resume made sure of that. Unfortunately, it also didn't take long to fall into old, familiar patterns. I tried to avoid it. I would go to work, then come home and play with my daughter until she would fall asleep. Then I would have to do all the shopping and other household stuff, since my wife had quickly fallen back in with the same crowd that we hung out with before I left for the Navy. It was as if we never left. I had a steady stream of tweakers parading through the house day and night, and the only thing she was interested in was getting high.

The house finally sold and my wife got a large sum of money. I found us an apartment that we could afford on my salary since she wasn't working, nor was she interested in contributing her inheritance to rent, and was able to move my step-daughter back in with us since she had been staying with her grandfather. I still struggled with my meth addiction. It was all around me and, as much as I would like to say I was able to resist, I did my share of it. But I struggled with it more than ever. Yes, it helped me get everything done because the wife wasn't doing much around the house. I was still doing most of the housework, all of the shopping, working full-time, and taking care of the baby when I was home. Since my daughter was the most important thing, I would wait until after she went to sleep for the night before going shopping. Since we didn't have a car and it was just over a mile to the store in each direction, I couldn't buy much so I would go almost nightly. Those shopping trips were my "alone time" and I could just be with my own thoughts, but that wasn't good. My thoughts were dark and depressing and scary. So I would always grab a couple of beers from the gas station on my way. I would drink one on the way to the store, and stash the other for the way back. Ironically, my wife, who was doing hundreds of dollars worth of meth daily, was complaining about how much I was drinking so I hid it from her whenever I could. So even though it meant walking two miles every night, I looked forward to these trips to the store.

Despite the fact that I was always surrounded by people, I was very lonely and depressed. I knew this wasn't the way I wanted to raise my daughter, but I didn't want to have another marriage fail.

What would that say about me? TWO marriages that didn't work out? So I gave it my best shot, and was probably one of the most co-dependent people on the planet. She would disappear sometimes for days at a time, staying at a local hotel, while I was stuck at home with the baby and having to call in sick. I really wanted things to work out, but no matter how screwed up in the head I was over everything that had happened, this was just taking things too far.

Finally, I moved out. I couldn't take the meth lifestyle any more. It wasn't how I wanted to raise my daughter, and it wasn't how I wanted to live my life. I had seen what a life without meth was like while I was in the Navy, and it was far better than where I was. So I gave my wife an ultimatum – meth or family. She chose the meth so I left.

I had nowhere to go but my father's. He was out of prison, and since my mother wasn't interested in letting me stay with her and I couldn't afford the rent on two places, I was forced to move in with him. He instantly fell into his old patterns, at one point telling me that he wished I was bisexual so we could have sex. Not exactly the kind of thing you want to hear from your own father. I stayed with him for three months while my custody case wound through the courts. Three months of him trying to get me to sleep with him. Three months of me thinking "My god, that really *is* all I am good for". I had gone full circle. I had gone from sex toy to drug addict, and back around.

So I focused on my daughter. She was the most important thing in the world to me, and I wasn't going to let her down. I couldn't bring her with me to my father's house - no way was I going to let him near her - so she stayed with her mother while I filed for emergency custody. I didn't know *what* I was going to do once I got custody, but I knew I needed it for her life…and for mine.

Finally, the day came when we had our custody hearing. I had filed for split legal and sole physical custody, based on a number of unsafe things that I had found when I visited her. The neglect she was suffering was horrifying. I would find her eating out of the garbage can; I watched her mother throw her plate of food on the floor for her to eat like she was a dog; her older sister and she would play outside, unsupervised, while mom had no idea where they were. In hindsight, I should have just taken her right then and there. I should have wrapped her in my arms and left, but I didn't. I didn't know what to do with her, or where to take her. Despite the fact that I had been doing most of the caring for her since I returned from the Navy, I didn't have the confidence that I could give her the proper care since I was working. Besides, I was still at my father's and that was out of the question. What was I supposed to do? Leave her with him while I went to work? I don't think so! So I brought all of this to the judge and begged him to let me take my daughter away.

Pam didn't even bother to show up to the hearing so not only was I awarded full physical custody, I was awarded sole legal custody. I was now the only person responsible for this two-year-old little girl.

Stunned and overwhelmed, I remember people congratulating me as I walked out of the courtroom. I had fought for this because I knew it was the right thing, but I wasn't ready for it. I was barely able to take care of myself, and now I had an almost two-year-old to take care of. Thankfully, my mother offered to let me stay with her now that I had my daughter with me. She wasn't doing it for me, but for her granddaughter. If it were just me, she'd have left me to figure it out myself. I didn't care, though. At least it was something. It was somewhere safe and I knew I wouldn't have to deal with my father trying to get me into his bed on a daily basis any longer.

As soon as we left the courthouse, we called the local police department in the city where my daughter was and requested assistance enforcing the custody order. I knew my wife wasn't going to just let me walk in and walk out with my daughter and the items needed. So two SWAT team members met us at the apartment and we went in with a bang. It was almost like an episode of the TV show *COPS.* As soon as she cracked the door, the officers shoved their way in and pushed her to a back room, while I scooped up my daughter and began gathering her belongings.

Pam wasn't going to let it go so easily. She fought and she made accusations and she pointed out that I had a felony warrant out of another state, but they stuck to what they were there for, and that was to make sure the custody order was followed and I was able to get what I needed.

For the next three days, my daughter sat at the front door of my mother's house and cried for her mommy. It was heartbreaking. Pam would come to the door late at night, after my daughter was asleep (thankfully), and we would turn her away. Finally, she got kicked out of the apartment for non-payment of rent. Which surprised me since she was withdrawing the max $300 per day from her account for drugs, yet she wasn't paying her rent. She appeared on our porch late one night asking for a place to stay.

I gave her a jacket and shut the door, both literally and figuratively. It was over for me. I'd had it and wasn't interested. I was off the meth and had a daughter to raise.

I still had my job, and had a co-worker whose daughter was the same age. He was also separated from his wife. I didn't want to live with my mother so the two of us got a place near work. I was off the meth, but I was making up for it with booze. My daughter always had the basics – clean clothes, food, a safe place to lay her head – but, emotionally, I wasn't able to give her my all. Sure, I would hold her, I would tell her I loved her, we would go do things, we would laugh and play, but I wasn't happy. Sometimes it was hard to even get out of bed and go to work. So, to fill that emptiness, I would drink. I tried going to counselling since I knew what had happened when I divorced my first wife. I didn't want to slip back into that deep state of depression and drugs again, not with my daughter depending on me, but I couldn't afford to go. I was barely making enough to pay for my rent, food, and daycare. What little money I did have left over pretty much went to beer.

Then one morning I woke up, but my daughter wouldn't. She had been sick for the previous five days and I had taken her to the doctor twice. He told me it was the flu and it would pass.

But it didn't.

That morning, I tried to wake her up, but she wouldn't respond. I tried to put her into a stroller to take her to the doctor, but she wouldn't sit up so I called an ambulance.

They arrived, took one look at her and said, "We have to go NOW." The urgency in their voice caused me to start to panic. They put her in the back of the ambulance and took off. I don't remember if they let me ride with them or whether I took a cab. This was my daughter, the little girl I loved more than anything in the world, the very thing that I do believe saved my life. Here she was unconscious and I didn't know why. The paramedics didn't know, either. When we got to the hospital, I tried to follow, but since the doctors didn't know what was wrong, they wouldn't let me in. Instead, they called CPS.

I was taken to a different room where the CPS worker told me that my daughter was likely going to die, but if she didn't die, they weren't going to let her go home with me. They were accusing me of neglect. They were telling me this was my fault!

My daughter was dying and I could do nothing about it. I felt totally helpless. I felt like I was going to explode. I had taken her to the doctor, I had taken the doctor's advice, I had done everything right, yet here they were telling me I had failed her, that I had killed the one thing that meant everything to me.

I was in shock. I couldn't breathe. I didn't know what to do.

Finally, the doctors figured it out. She had developed Type 1 diabetes and was in a coma due to extremely high blood sugar. They were able to give her insulin and stabilize her. She was going to live, after all.

The CPS worker didn't seem too happy. She contacted our pediatrician and verified my story that I *had* actually been to the doctor twice in the previous five days. That I *had* followed his advice. That I had *not* neglected my daughter. So she had no basis to take my daughter from me. For some reason that seemed to make her unhappy. She "broke" the news to me that they wouldn't be taking my daughter from me, although she told me they would be watching me. I felt very small, but my heart was huge. My daughter was going to live. I didn't care about anything else.

She spent the next four days in a coma. I knew she would be okay when the nurses tried to brush her hair and she would squirm. She always hated having her hair brushed. She wouldn't react to being pricked with a needle, but the hair brushing? Yeah, she'd be okay.

I was overwhelmed, though. I was barely keeping it together before. How was I supposed to take care of a three-year-old diabetic that needed regular insulin shots? I had a crash course in nutrition, nursing, how to give injections, how to read blood sugars. It was all so overwhelming that I was in overload. She had lapsed into the coma on July 3rd. I stayed by her bedside for 36 hours before the nurses convinced me to go home and get some sleep. I spent the night of that 4th of July sitting in my apartment, watching the fireworks, and drinking beer after beer after beer, totally overwhelmed and wondering just what the hell I was going to do now…

7

"Living in a daydream, only place I had to stay."

– Ozzy Osbourne, *Over the Mountain*

As a child, I had developed certain survival "skills" to help me deal with the abuse. These helped quite a bit by removing me from reality so I didn't have to face what was happening. Because of the regularity of the abuse, that way of living just became the norm for me.

Which was helpful when I was young, but not so much as an adult.

I had never really learned to live. I had just been surviving day to day, never really allowing myself to experience life. And without experiences, you can't really learn anything. So when I found myself responsible not only for an almost three-year-old child, but one that had a life threatening illness, it was a bit overwhelming. Between an incestuous, pedophile father and an emotionally distant, alcoholic mother, I didn't really have any parenting role models to speak of so I didn't have those experiences to pull from, either. I was lost and scared, and I began to withdraw even further. I couldn't handle my own life before this happened. This was overwhelming, to say the least.

The coma lasted for four days, and my daughter was in the hospital a total of eight. It was the longest eight days that I had ever experienced. I spent half of that time sitting at her bedside, reading to her and holding her hand. The other half of the time I spent back at my apartment, sitting in the dark. I couldn't sleep, I couldn't think straight, I didn't know what to do – so I drank. A lot. Ever since I started drinking in 8th grade, that had been how I had handled my problems. Since I wasn't doing the drugs anymore, I doubled up on the alcohol.

My mother was regularly at the hospital, too. Not as much as I was, but she did spend quite a bit of time there. I was glad she was there. It was really the only way that I was okay with not being by my daughter's bedside. After all, I didn't want my daughter there alone.

At one point, my father showed up to visit. He was understandably worried for both my daughter and me. Where my mother was emotionally cold and distant, my father was warm and caring. Unlike with my mother, with him you got the feeling he really loved and cared about you. However, his presence didn't sit well with my mother, who was still very angry with him for what he had done to my sister. As I walked him towards the hospital exit after his visit, we were confronted by two police officers who proceeded to arrest him on the spot. He was still on parole and wasn't supposed to be around children so my mother used that opportunity to send him back to prison. It was pretty upsetting and, I felt, uncalled for. After all, it wasn't as though he was doing anything other than being supportive. He wasn't threatening, and when I saw the fear in his eyes as he was being arrested, knowing that he was heading back to prison, I felt really bad for him, and really angry at my mother. Here I was, barely holding it together with my daughter in the hospital. My father shows up, being more emotionally supportive than my mother, and she has him arrested out of spite. It didn't sit well with me. Legally, she did the right thing, I suppose. After all, he *was* in violation of his parole. But she acted selfishly and spitefully, and that certainly didn't help make things easier.

Finally, the day came when my daughter was being released. Thankfully, my mom offered to let us move back in with her. She had stopped drinking by this point, and I think she could see how overwhelmed I was by all of this. She definitely knew I was drinking too much. Whether she thought that this would help me stop, I don't know. In fact, I really don't know what she was thinking. We didn't really talk much, certainly not about anything important. I didn't want to go back and live with her again. I didn't like her much. In fact, I was still really mad about what she had said so many years prior when she blamed me for what my father had been doing to me.

Perhaps she thought I had been doing it willingly. After all, I was about 15 at the time, and that would be the natural assumption. But I don't think she realized how long it had gone on, how many times it had happened, how strongly I had been conditioned to accept it and allow it to happen. I try not to blame her for not understanding. I don't really get it myself, even today.

But that wedge between us didn't help things. Yes, we had a safe place to be. Yes, that took a lot of pressure off and, deep down, I was happy I wouldn't have to do this alone. But I was so incredibly overwhelmed by what I was having to learn and do with regards to caring for a three-year-old insulin dependent diabetic that I didn't have time to think about how lucky we were.

Having lived like an emotionless robot for so many years had its perks. Looking back, there were many times that I should have been heartbroken or sad. People I was close to would die and my gut reaction was along the lines of "Meh, it happens". Women would reject me and I would just see it as nothing to get upset about. After all, I wasn't like the other guys. I was worthless and didn't have a lot going for me. Why *would* they choose me?

So I was always surprised when they did.

It's funny. I had some friends that joked about my dating style, saying my pickup lines must have gone something like "Hi, I'm Steve. You're cute. Let's get married". But that really wasn't my approach at all. I didn't go into relationships with the intent of getting married. I just needed somebody in my life. I did not like being alone, and even though caring about people wasn't "safe", deep down I needed somebody to care about me. Finally, I met somebody that seemed like a good fit.

We dated several times before the hospital incident and that almost broke us up. I think it was too much drama for her, and I understood that. I certainly was too overwhelmed at that point to have any energy to put into a relationship but, on the other hand, it was a great escape. Once my daughter and I got settled in at my mother's house, we picked up dating again. Slowly to be sure, since my primary focus was on my daughter at that point, but enough to keep things going.

And I guess I didn't have enough going on in my life at that time because between living with my mother who I was really angry at (and not just a superficial anger, but one that started deep down inside), raising a special needs three-year-old who really missed her mother and didn't understand why her father was jabbing her with needles six times a day, and trying to keep it all together and keep my job, I managed to get my girlfriend pregnant.

Seriously? As if I needed *more* on my plate. Of course, the more overwhelmed I got, the more I withdrew inside my head. I didn't freak out or have any breakdowns or anything like that. I would just react to the pressure by switching on my auto-pilot and living life day to day, minute to minute, as robotically and methodically as I could. I had no real emotions. I had been turned into a shell of a person. Sure, there were times when I really, *really* wanted to have feelings. I would watch movies where people would have these intense emotional situations, and wish I could experience those. I would long for something to come along and shake me out of my cold, hard shell. But that just didn't happen. Sure, I had lots of things going on that most people would probably say were rather emotional, but I didn't feel it. I couldn't handle it all so I shut down and didn't handle any of it. But there was something different about this woman, some special connection that I felt that was different from the others. There was something about her that put me at ease and made me comfortable. She was intelligent and funny and beautiful. But more than that, she was just plain awesome. While the pregnancy kind of freaked me out at first, I quickly began to embrace it. Perhaps this was the change that would turn things around…a new baby, a wonderful woman to share my life with. I needed this. But more than that, I wanted it.

Four months into the pregnancy, we got married. My mother was against it and, since she couldn't talk me out of it, she tried to talk my fiancé out of it. She told her all the horror stories she could think of, such as how I was emotionally not ready, how I had ruined my credit to the point where it would take years to dig myself out, etc. She threw every bad thing she could think of at her, but my fiancé didn't listen. She saw my mother as a manipulative woman trying to control my life. She couldn't figure out why, though. She got the feeling that my mother had some deep issues with me, that there was something really off about the way she felt towards me, that there was nothing "motherly" about the way she treated me.

So we got married and I moved in with her, bringing my daughter and all of my emotional baggage with me.

I did start drinking less, though. As withdrawn and emotionless as I was, there was something different, something special about this woman. Co-dependency aside, there was something about her that filled a hole in me. She was thoughtful, she was kind. She loved me despite my past, and I was finding that I didn't need to escape quite so often. I quit my job and found another one that paid more, and was closer to home. I started getting my act together, much like I had when I first joined the military. Life was finally falling into place, and I was happy. I finally had somebody who truly loved me. I had one beautiful daughter and another on the way. I had beaten the odds.

When my second daughter was born, I couldn't have been happier. Just as my oldest daughter was my "welcome home" baby, this one was my "new hope" baby. Things were different, things were better, life seemed so much more hopeful and solid. Things weren't perfect by a long shot, at least not inside my head, but I seemed to have it all. At least it looked that way to the outside world. I had a beautiful, loving wife, two beautiful daughters, a good job. For somebody who didn't have a college education, I seemed to have managed to put together a pretty good life that I was proud of, but that was only on the outside. Inside my head, I was more scared than ever. I had no idea how to be a father, no idea how to be a husband, no idea how to be myself. I was clinging to a dream, a fantasy that everything would just work itself out. I didn't have a clue what I was doing, but I was good at hiding that. I felt disconnected from reality, as if the real me was inside a bubble, trapped inside the shell of a person that others saw. A bubble that I couldn't escape from, didn't *want* to escape from, at least not completely since I knew that the bubble was preventing me from releasing all the darkness and anger that raged deep inside. Since I didn't know how to release just the good parts of the real me, I had to keep all of it buried.

I loved going home at the end of the day and holding my daughter while I took a nap. She was so tiny, so beautiful, so perfect. It was such a wonderful way to end the day, with my baby daughter sleeping on my chest while I laid there, decompressing. It was comforting and nice, but it did little to help me break out of my shell. I wanted to be a different person so bad. Not a person with a different life, but simply a different person who could fully appreciate what he had. But no matter how hard I tried, I always found myself banging against that wall I had put up. The wall that held back the darkness also kept out the light. I couldn't release one without the other, and I didn't dare free the darkness so I learned to live without the light.

Unknown to us at the time, the traumatic experiences that my older daughter had experienced at such a young age had impacted her development. Much like my abuse had impacted the way I saw the world, being neglected by her mother, then torn away from her the way she was, followed within the year by an eight day hospital stay, caused her brain to wire itself into survival mode, as well. Even though she had me by her side, she developed issues that she would later overcome, but would definitely impact our lives throughout her childhood.

She missed her mother, there was never any question about that. Despite all of the neglect and horrific conditions she had to endure, they had somehow bonded like mothers and their children tend to do. She always had this fantasy in her head that her mother was rich, famous, and coming any day to take her back. It couldn't have been further from the truth, of course, but she wasn't open to allowing anybody else to slip into that role. So no matter how hard my wife tried to mother her and care for her, she wasn't having it. She would totally reject every little thing my wife tried. I would go to work and my wife, who was too pregnant to work, would try to read to her and play with her, but my daughter just wasn't interested. All she wanted to do was go to preschool and play with her friends, which was understandable, but it was hard on my wife to be constantly rejected. Day after day, time after time, every effort to bond was shut down. She was a mini-me. She seemed to have many of the same emotional issues as I had – cold, distant, and needing to keep things under control. I don't know much of this was actually due to her childhood trauma, and how much of it might have been because we tend to emulate our parents. Just as my mother was no role model for emotional intimacy, I have to think that my coldness and emotional black-hole had some effect on my daughter. It isn't a nice thought to think that your inability to bond emotionally with your child would teach them the same coping skills, but it is a reality. The trauma I experienced as a child had more far-reaching consequences than just my life.

Strangely enough, many years later, her trauma would lay the groundwork for our healing.

8

"The wreckage of my past keeps haunting me. It just won't leave me alone."

– Ozzy Osbourne, *Road to Nowhere*

I spent so many years perfecting my balancing act between what was going on inside my head and what I showed to the real world that it had become second nature. I was able to charm people into thinking I cared even though, deep down inside, I couldn't care less. I was able to keep the horrible memories at bay. I was working as an IT consultant at the time, dealing with dozens of clients on a regular basis. They all loved me and the work I did for them, and it was nice to feel wanted and liked, and being out there helped me ignore the torment inside. Not unlike the drugs and alcohol, working was a great escape. These people didn't know my history and I had become excellent at hiding it. I liked being the person they thought I was, even though I wasn't that person at all. I had developed a nice little wall around my feelings and emotions which protected me from all the hurt, anger, and sadness that years of abuse had given me. Internally, I had fine-tuned all sorts of ways to protect my mind from the horrors of what had happened, but it wasn't easy. It took a lot of effort to maintain that balance. Subconscious effort to be sure, but it was a lot of effort and there wasn't much room for anything else. It seemed that I walked a wobbly path between normalcy and madness, but I was able to hold it together somehow.

Until my daughter turned five.

Not unlike the first time my father had sex with me, I remember a particular moment with complete clarity. I was standing in the kitchen with my daughter between me and the door to the hallway. The sunlight was shining through the window behind me. The innocence of my daughter couldn't be denied, and that was when it hit me. That's how old I was when my father began having sex with me.

The sweetness, the innocence, the awesomeness of a five-year-old child, and my father had taken all that away and turned me into a shell of a human. He had taken a smart, funny, inquisitive boy and turned him into a withdrawn, self-loathing, full of anger and hate, drug addict and alcoholic. Who would do that? What kind of monster would do that to an innocent child?

That's when I snapped.

I didn't snap like the people you see in the news. I didn't go on a killing spree or a crime spree, but that wall I had so carefully built, that line I had been teetering on for so long, all of that started to come crashing down and I could almost feel myself spiraling out of control.

I couldn't deal with anything any longer. Any sort of fighting or arguing between my wife and daughter was too much – I couldn't handle it. Dealing with my clients for work was too much – I couldn't handle them. Having to report back to my employer was too much. Every little thing was just too much. All those years of being able to control things and compartmentalize them, all those years of focusing on simply surviving and not letting the outside world in had left me unable to deal with everything flooding me at once. The pressure of it all was crushing me. The pressure was threatening to break down that wall I had built. The wall that protected me from all the bad things, and the bad feelings, and the scary stuff.

I couldn't have that wall break. I would not survive. I had to do whatever it took to keep that wall intact. Nobody understood what was behind it. I didn't even know what was in there. All I knew was that it was dark and scary and dangerous, and it needed to be kept locked away at any cost.

So I held it at bay by trying to drown it with alcohol. I fought the pressure of the outside world by withdrawing into my head even further, and even though I loved my wife more than anything, I avoided contact with her and my daughters because they would elicit feelings in me and I had no more room in there. I was ready to explode.

I panicked and ran. I left my wife and youngest daughter, somehow convincing my mother to let me and my oldest daughter temporarily move in with her. How I managed to convince her, I don't know. I don't believe she felt this was the right thing for me so maybe she allowed it out of guilt for not having protected me. I had gotten half-apologies from her over the years so I do believe she felt bad about what happened. Maybe that was her motivation. I don't know. We still didn't talk – at least not about this. She had dropped clues that she had a similar story from her childhood, but not to the same extent. Regardless, she provided a safe haven for my daughter while I emotionally freaked out. Whether it was noticeable to others or not, I don't know, but I was in complete meltdown mode. I busied myself with a girlfriend, who I started talking to after my wife and I separated and who lived 100 miles away, a distance that felt safe – both figuratively and literally. I was in overdrive. I was drinking as much as humanly possible while still holding down a job. I was able to provide the basics for my daughter, but I did so robotically. I took her to school, I went to work, I picked her up from school, we had dinner. We would stiffly hug each other before she left for school and when I would pick her up. I would try to read to her at night but, for some reason, I didn't have it in me. I knew she deserved a warm, loving parent and I wanted to be real. I wanted to love and laugh and be happy, but I couldn't. There was no room for that in my head. I was barely holding it together. I couldn't do this emotion thing. I didn't know how, and I felt that if I even let the tiniest emotion out from behind the wall I had built, it would all come crashing down. So rather than actual human interaction, I found myself getting lost in a world online. I found that while I craved relationships with people, nearby ones were too dangerous. Too risky. Too painful. So I fell in with an interesting online crowd.

I had been participating in Usenet for a couple of years at this point. If you aren't familiar with Usenet, it's basically a global online bulletin board – the predecessor to today's forums that you find everywhere. It was the wild side of the Internet. There were no moderators, unless you specifically went to a moderated group, and there were no rules. I started out in a hacking-related group, alt.2600, and learned a lot about the darker side of the Internet. I learned how to steal passwords, I learned how to abuse the weaknesses in most computer operating systems, I learned how to do "recon" of a network and find holes without arousing suspicion. But, even better, I learned about – and perfected – "Social Engineering", which really is nothing more than the ability to convince people that you are who you want them to think you are. It's really a glorified name for an expert bullshitter, but I had a knack for it. All of my years of learning to read people, figuring out what they want, then using that information to keep myself safe while getting what I wanted seems to have been preparing me for becoming a big online bullshitter. You might think "Meh, what's the big deal?", but it was a skill that came in super handy, especially once I found the next online group that was going to keep me busy for the next couple of years…Alt.Hackers.Malicious.

A.H.M was a fun place. It was like the wild west of the Internet. When I arrived, I just sat and watched, learning who the players were, watching how they interacted. When I did finally jump in, I was ready to join the fun. Where alt.2600 discussed ways to exploit weaknesses in computers and networks, A.H.M acted on that information. Where alt.2600 had unspoken rules about black-hat, or illegal, activities, A.H.M encouraged them. It sort of felt like leaving a party at Chuck-E-Cheeses and stepping into somebody's 21st birthday party – it was loud, it was wild, it was fun.

We would have "war games" where somebody would put a system online, and everybody would try to break into it. First one to retrieve "the flag" would win bragging rights. Those who won, like myself, were bumped up in status in the group. But we didn't stop there. The people that would stop by that weren't liked would find their own systems compromised and, sometimes, destroyed. We would steal their emails, we would deface their websites – A.H.M was to the digital world what punk rock was to the real world. It was a big "Screw you. We'll do it our way" type of place and I loved it. I didn't have a problem joining in with the shenanigans at all. It gave me power, it gave me control.

But better than that was that it gave me an escape. The beauty of online communication is that you can do it without being emotional. You can have relationships that aren't nearly as risky and, in a place with no real rules such as A.H.M, you can get angry at somebody, "spank" them, then move on after getting your anger out.

And "spank" people we did.

It wasn't uncommon at all for people to jump into the group without having learned who was who and what was what. They would say the wrong thing, or pick on the wrong person, and we would go after them like sharks in a feeding frenzy. I'm not talking about people who were obviously just too stupid to figure out the game, but those people that were intentionally mean and nasty. Yes, the name of the group had the word "malicious" in it, but that referred to our behavior towards computers and networks, not each other. But people got back what they gave. If they came in with a chip on their shoulder, they usually left with that chip stuffed somewhere that the sun doesn't shine.

We were "friends" as much as people could be who didn't really know each other outside of their nicknames and behaviors. But perhaps, unlike some groups, we didn't *want* to know each other's real names. If one of us was to get caught, it was safer not to know who the other people were.

But that didn't mean we weren't quick to uncover the people that we didn't like behind the masks. I became really good at digging up people's real identities. Although sometimes it was just easier to hack into their computer and look through their documents folder for resumes or other identifying information, I found I could spend hours following people's digital footprints to uncover the real them. It was a skill that required patience and determination, two things I seemed to have an abundance of online. Usually, once you "outted" their real identity, they would slink away quickly, never to be seen again. People hate to be exposed on the Internet. For one thing, it's embarrassing, but another reason is that there are many, many crazy kooks out there that won't hesitate to use that information against you. There are people out there that would happily ruin your life for no reason other than that they can, but we weren't those people.

Unless you were a predator.

I don't remember exactly how it all started, but there was a core group of us that somehow ended up deciding that we were going to use our knowledge and skills for good, or at least what we considered good. We began going after online predators, usually men who were trolling for sex with children. This was before "To Catch A Predator" came along and, although the general idea was similar, we didn't have the legal restraints that the TV show did. They had to follow the law and do things on the up and up. We didn't have that issue. We didn't care about the law. We only wanted to find them and expose the sick bastards.

And find and expose we did. The most successful method we used, but not the only one, was to break into mail servers, read all the emails stored there, redirect all future emails to us, and then go after those people that were undoubtedly looking for sex with children. We would respond to their emails to gather more information, dig for information on the Internet, and put together a package which we would then turn over to the police...anonymously, of course. After all, we didn't want some highly paid defense attorney to discover where and how that information had been collected. We didn't want to risk the predator getting out of doing prison time because of how we had discovered his activities. Since some of the organizations we hit were somewhat high profile, we stayed in the shadows as much as we possibly could.

Besides, we didn't want it to be about us. To most of us, the children that were being saved were the focus of the project, not our own fame. We weren't doing this so we could say "Look at what we're doing". We did it because we hated predators and we were more effective when working in secret. That isn't to say that *all* of us kept quiet. We did have one person who ran a blog where he would post the details of what we were accomplishing. He seemed to enjoy his bragging rights and that was okay. On one or two occasions, we would only have a photo and an email of the person, but couldn't quite track them down so he would post it on his blog. The person would find it and email him some nasty email about whatever, and we would take those email headers and track that person down, which we wouldn't have been able to do if he hadn't sent that email so it all worked out for us.

It also allowed us to go back and look at some of the things we had accomplished during those times when we just didn't feel like doing it anymore. I don't know the background of the people I was working with on that project – heck, I don't even know all of their real names – but for me, while my abuse background was a driving force in getting me into the project, it also made it incredibly difficult to keep it up after a while. Having to immerse myself into that culture of predators took a lot out of me. Dealing with those people and listening to their twisted justifications and the excuses they made to themselves about how it wasn't just okay what they were doing, but actually beneficial to the child just made me sick.

It wasn't just me, either. After a while, the person maintaining the blog seemed to have lost focus and gotten super paranoid about things that were unrelated to the project. Other people involved started putting less and less effort into it. I stopped altogether. The mental and emotional toll was just too great. Sure, it was nice to be able to have that project to focus on because it took my mind off of what was happening in the real world. It was nice to know that we helped rescue eight autistic children from their predatory "teacher" who had created a school just so he could abuse them. That predator went on to be convicted and sent to prison. His roommate, who was also involved, committed suicide. I have asked myself many times if I was bothered by the fact that what we did was the catalyst for that suicide.

I have decided that no, not only do I not really care, I would do it again in a heartbeat. Sometimes we would have people send us money, thinking they were joining an organization that supported sex between men and boys. We'd spend that money on beer or whatever, but I couldn't keep it up. Fun or not, it deepened my depression. It prevented me from spending quality time with my own children. It kept me from living my own life. It prevented me from getting better and working on the issues that I needed to work on.

I had been "lost" for a couple of years this time around. I was in the depths of a major depression. Sure, I would get up and go to work, but I was still nothing more than a shell of a person. My daughter was suffering because I couldn't be there emotionally. I couldn't manage to keep myself grounded in reality. Everything and everybody irritated me. I just wanted to be left alone, and that wasn't fair. It wasn't fair to my wife, it wasn't fair to my daughters, it wasn't fair to me. My father was still controlling me and preventing me from living my life. The abuse was over, but I couldn't get rid of its effects. He had raped *me,* but my daughters and wife were still suffering its after-effects. How was this fair to them? They had done nothing to deserve this. My wife was not to blame for what happened, and my children were not even born when it happened so why did they have to suffer because of what he did to me?

We tend to think of abuse affecting only those that are abused. But the sad reality is that it also affects everybody they come into contact with, sometimes for the rest of their lives. I had my childhood stolen from me and, as a result, my daughters had their childhoods affected. I saw this happening and didn't want them to suffer. I didn't want *their* children to suffer, either. I saw this and decided nobody but me could stop it.

When my father was in prison, they used our family history to point out how abuse is handed down from generation to generation. I was beaten and raped by him, he was beaten by his father, who was beaten by his father, who was likely beaten by his father. And so on and so on back through the generations.

I have never beaten my children. I just don't have that in me. Sure, I have swatted them on the butt, but I have never beaten them. I know, I know. There are some people that think any sort of physical contact is just as horrifying as a "beating", but whatever. You can have your parenting methods and I will have mine, as bad as they were. I certainly have never, and *would* never, sexually abuse them. But I wasn't exactly the loving parent I wanted to be. Because I never learned how to touch without it being sexual, I didn't hug my children enough. I didn't put my arm around them and tell them I loved them. I just wasn't "there" for them. So while I wasn't physically or sexually abusing them, I realized I wasn't the type of parent I wanted to be. I wasn't the type of parent they needed me to be. I wasn't the type of parent a child deserves.

And I wasn't okay with that. I had looked into my daughter's eyes and felt her pain. It was time, I decided, to make a change. To take away the power of the abuse, to remove the roadblocks to being a decent parent, to rebuild my life.

9

"I'm just a lonely soul who's trying to find some peace of mind."

– Black Sabbath, *Piece of Mind*

After so many years of being "on the run" emotionally, I was tired of running. I was tired of living inside my head at the expense of my life and the lives of those around me. My daughters counted on me, my wife loved me. I needed to be there for them and I wasn't able to be. They were the best thing to ever happen to me and I just couldn't be there with them. Not with the mindset I was in. I was sick and tired of living in the past, of letting my father still control me. I needed to take back that control if I was ever going to be the parent my children deserved.

So I made a decision that I was going to get better. I worked things out with my wife and my daughter, left my mother's and moved back. With the help of my wife, I found some free counseling through the San Francisco Child Abuse Prevention Council. Even though I knew I was not a threat to my children, my history was such that I was considered a "high risk" for perpetuating that abuse so they provided me with free counseling. Of course, free comes at a cost. The therapist I was to meet with was an intern and hadn't even finished her training yet, but that didn't bother me. I was determined to heal myself. I didn't care about the therapist. She was just my guide. I would be doing all the work.

I started off ready to go. I knew it would probably take me about a year and things would be different. I may not be totally healed in that time, but there would be a huge improvement that everybody would notice, and life would be totally different and better.

Thankfully, I got a really good intern on my first shot. Something about her put me at ease and I was ready to go. I wanted to heal and knew that all I had to do was admit what happened and the healing could begin.

Except it wasn't that easy.

At first, I couldn't even get the words out. She asked why I was there and I told her it was because I wanted to be a better parent. That was easy enough to say, but when it came time to talk about the abuse, it wasn't so easy. I physically could not get the words to come out. My throat would close up, my sinuses would clog up, my chest would tighten and it was all I could do to make sure I was breathing.

Keeping what happened a secret had been such a part of my life that my subconscious just couldn't let it out that easily. I was in a fight with my own brain and body. Despite my consciousness knowing that I needed to get this out into the open so I could move past it, my subconscious had been trained over the years to protect that information at any cost, and it wasn't about to let any of it go without a fight. I struggled and it finally happened: "My father sexually abused me."

It was the first time I had told anybody other than my wives and sisters, people who I felt safe with. I didn't know how she was going to react. I felt awkward and vulnerable. I felt exposed and naked and humiliated.

But she didn't say anything. We just sat there in silence for a while and I began to tell her my story.

When I looked up, she was crying.

I honestly was not sure how to feel about that. I figured it was maybe because she was an intern and wasn't used to hearing about bad things. It wasn't as though my story was all that horrible, was it? I mean, I had survived. I could think of many things that were much worse than what I had gone through.

Over the years, I would have two more therapists moved to tears when I told them the detailed story of my childhood, and these weren't interns, either. They were experienced therapists with years of listening to people's stories, yet they found themselves moved to tears upon hearing mine? After years of just accepting my childhood, I just have never managed to find the total tragedy in it. It was what it was.

But at the time, I just thought it was odd that she would have tears running down her cheeks. For some reason, that didn't scare me off. I stuck with her now that I had finally opened up about my childhood. I had told somebody and they hadn't run away screaming. They hadn't called me a freak or a sicko, and they didn't make me feel like something was wrong with me. I felt as though a weight had been lifted off my chest and I wanted more of that feeling.

As an intern, she was only supposed to work there for a year before heading off to somewhere else, but she stuck with me for three years. Three years of weekly visits. Three years of hard work. There were many times that I didn't want to go. Many times I just wanted to pull off into a parking lot and sit there for an hour before going home, but I didn't. I had this incredible opportunity to fix things and I didn't want to just blow it off so I went. And we talked. And talked. And talked. Sometimes we didn't talk about anything heavy because I couldn't do that week after week. But sometimes we went to those dark places inside me. Sometimes things got so intense that the air felt heavy. Frequently, I would find that my body would fight back. I would realize that I wasn't breathing, or I would get really bad headaches. Sometimes, when we would peel back that darkness and try to peek inside, I would suddenly and completely forget what we were talking about, or I would find myself disassociating and feeling like I was outside of my body. It was very strange the different ways and lengths that my body would go just to protect what I had hidden down inside me.

One night, after a particularly intense session, I arrived home and my wife looked at me funny and asked what was wrong with my face. It didn't look right. And she was right. Half of my face had frozen. I don't think it was a coincidence that I had delved into some very intense memories at my therapy session earlier that evening. We were stirring up memories that my brain had worked very hard to suppress, and bringing those to light was wreaking havoc with my nervous system.

My face stayed half-frozen for four days, but I didn't let that stop me. We continued on with the therapy…sometimes making progress, other times just sitting in silence. I found the silence comforting. I was able to sit with my thoughts and let them roll over me. I had nothing else to worry about during that hour – no kids, no wife, no work – so I just let my mind deal with little chunks of darkness at a time.

One night, I asked her if I was crazy. I had to know. I certainly felt crazy. So much seemed wrong with me. I had so much darkness and despair that it just couldn't be normal. I mean, I knew I wasn't like everybody else, I had obvious issues for obvious reasons, but I just wanted to know. She didn't want to put a label on me, but I pushed. Finally, she laid it all out and told me that the symptoms I had described to her were indicative of Borderline Personality Disorder. That if I insisted on a formal diagnosis, it was going to be PTSD and BPD, both later confirmed by a psychiatrist. She said that she didn't want to give me a diagnosis because she felt I might focus on that and not treat the whole package. But I was okay with that. In fact, I was better than okay. I was almost happy to have that as my diagnosis. It meant that I wasn't crazy after all. For all these years, I had felt so crazy and out of control that nobody could ever relate to where I was coming from, that nobody could possibly understand. Heck, even *I* couldn't understand most of the time. Yet there was a name for it. If there was a name, people had dealt with it before, and not just a few times. It had to be somewhat common for it to have a name. So, to me, this was great news. It didn't change how I felt about myself, but it did give me hope. A hope that we could move towards understanding. A hope that we could move towards healing.

Finally, after we had been doing this for three years, my therapist moved on to continue her career. I was still haunted by my past. We had done a lot of groundwork, and I was able to see how much work I still needed to do. We had pulled the covers off the darkness and peeked inside, but I wasn't much closer to being "healed". There was just far too much down inside me that had to be dealt with. We weren't talking about something that happened a few times. I was trying to come to grips with my entire childhood, with week after week and year after year of repeated abuse. I was trying to make sense of so much that I needed more time.

About two years into my initial run of therapy, I had decided to quit smoking so I talked with my doctor and she prescribed Welbutrin, an anti-depressant that is also commonly used to help with the nicotine cravings. About a month into taking it, I began to notice something. The sky seemed a bit bluer. The sun a bit more warm. The dark cloud that followed me everywhere was not nearly as intense. I went to a psychiatrist and told him everything that was going on. He was only there for medication management, not therapy since I was still seeing my therapist at the time. He confirmed both the PTSD and Borderline Personality Disorder diagnoses, and added a couple more…generalized anxiety and major depression. I didn't feel these diagnoses were as cool as the first two, but they certainly made sense.

We upped the dosage of the anti-depressants which helped but, although they took the edge off, they never quite got rid of the dark cloud that seemed to go everywhere with me. They never silenced the demons inside me. They helped, but I needed more.

When my first therapist moved on, I got another intern. She didn't work for me so I got another. And another. And another. But none of them worked for me. I got tired of explaining myself over and over. I got tired of telling the story of my childhood. I mean, it did get easier. Each time I told it, it took away a little bit of its power over me, but I never managed to get into the groove of healing. I tried for two more years, but just couldn't get back on track.

But I had already opened Pandora's Box. There was no closing the door on what I had seen inside myself. I knew I needed to deal with it before it ate me alive, but with no guide to help me through that journey, I turned to the one thing that had helped me thus far. I started stepping up the drinking again.

I had never stopped drinking during those three years of therapy, but I wasn't getting drunk every day, either. Having that therapeutic release helped keep the demons at bay so I didn't need the alcohol. But now I found myself in an almost worse spot than before. Now I *knew* what was in there. I knew where those demons were and what they were about, and I didn't have any way to deal with them. The proverbial barn door had been opened, and the horses weren't going back in peacefully. With no outlet to speak of, I quickly slipped back into old patterns.

I struggled and struggled to stop drinking. I had been going to Alcoholics Anonymous since I was a teenager, but never for me – always for my mother. She had been after me to quit for as long as I could remember, but I never got anything out of it so I didn't go back on my own. It just wasn't my thing. I wasn't drinking every day. I could go two or three days without it sometimes. But when I was drinking, I was drinking more and more. I had upset the equilibrium of my life by digging into that darkness. Whereas before I felt like I was teetering on the edge of a cliff, about to fall into madness and despair at any time, I now felt like I was still on that edge, but my demons were grasping at my ankles, trying to pull me over.

And, one day, they did.

10

"Never say die."

– Black Sabbath, *Never Say Die*

I was, once again, at the point where I couldn't handle any additional stress. Every little thing would overwhelm me. I was at my breaking point. I was the camel with an overloaded back and, one day, the straw came down and I just snapped. Despite the fact that my wife had been there for me and had been so supportive, despite the fact that I had never felt as safe anywhere as I did with her, I packed up my bags, grabbed my oldest daughter, rented a small apartment, and moved. I needed to get away from all the horror and darkness of my life and, for some reason, I thought that running away from it all would work. I don't know *why* I thought that. I had been doing that for years and it had never helped, but I wasn't able to think clearly. I couldn't focus on anything except my job. All of my relationships were suffering because I couldn't put any energy or effort into them. My home life was falling apart, I had no social life, I wasn't seeing a therapist anymore, and I was quickly losing my mind.

I had to drink. It was the only thing that was keeping me sane. I was drinking in the morning, I was drinking at noon, I was drinking all night long. When I wasn't drinking, I was sitting in darkness... literally and figuratively. I just wanted to be left alone. I wanted everybody to go away. I didn't want to be bothered with anything or anybody. I had never felt so overwhelmed by despair and darkness before. I just didn't care anymore.

I just wanted to sit in a dark room and drink myself to death.

But I couldn't. I had a wife and daughters who loved me, who needed me. I had sisters who loved me. I had people who cared. I knew all of this, but it wasn't enough. I was tired of fighting, tired of fending off my demons, tired of wondering why my father had done this to me. Hadn't I been a good son? What had I done to deserve all of this? Why me? Why couldn't I have been one of the lucky ones? Why was I so undeserving of a "normal" childhood? Why did I have to have *him* as my father? I didn't have the answers. Nobody had the answers. But that didn't matter. I had to beat this for my children. I didn't want them to have similar questions when they grew up. I didn't want them to sit in a dark room and wonder "why". I didn't want them to grow up without a father.

I wish I could say that I made my decision and turned it all around on the spot, but it wasn't that simple. I struggled for months in the depths of that depressive episode. I drank from morning to night. I sat in front of the TV, watching the flickering images cross the screen with no idea what I was watching. I was a shell of a person, dead and emotionless inside. I was still taking my anti-depressants, but they were no match for the copious amounts of alcohol that I was drowning myself in.

It took a few months, but the intensity of the depression finally began to lift. I was still very, very depressed and drinking far more than any one person should be able to and still function. But function

I did. Despite the fact that I spent every lunch hour in the bar, despite the fact that I spent every night with a bottle in hand, I somehow managed to keep on functioning at work and at home. Then I got laid off from my job. It was 2008, the economy was suffering, and companies were cutting back everywhere they could. Since I was the latest hire for my department, I was the first to be cut. I could no longer afford to live apart from my family and, deep down, I was glad about this turn of events. I had wanted to get back together with my wife, but was too depressed and embarrassed to approach her about it. But now I had no choice. I was being forced into it.

Thankfully, she was open to the idea and allowed me to return. Things had been bad between her and my oldest before we left, but they agreed to work on that, just as I agreed to work on myself and my relationships. We could do this.

I think that as a way to avoid my own issues, I began looking at my oldest daughter. She had suffered some pretty bad trauma as an infant due to her mother being a meth addict, neglect, and removal from the home. We had known all along that this was the driving force for the issues between her and her stepmother, but I was determined to fix it.

So I began researching. I began reading and talking with nurses and doctors and therapists. I found an online support group for parents of children with attachment issues, and it all began to click and fall into place. But for every tidbit I learned about my daughter, I learned something about myself. I, too, was a child of trauma. Like my daughter, I had experienced things that had changed the way my brain had wired itself during development. Like my daughter, this had affected the way I related to people. My marriages, my parenting, my friendships (or lack thereof) were all affected by this trauma. The fact that I was always on edge – a result of constantly being under stress as a child. The fact that I was cold and emotionless – a result of my childhood trauma. I could trace it all back. I could see the link. I could see the cure.

Okay, I couldn't see the cure. I wish I could, but I was at a loss. If my brain had hard-wired itself in a certain way, how can that be fixed? How are you going to go in and re-wire your brain? That's crazy talk. So I began to accept the fact that some things just were the way they were. That they weren't going to change, but that didn't mean I couldn't change the things that were possible to change. I couldn't physically re-wire my brain, but I *could* be aware of how it was affecting my life and my relationships, then try to adjust my behavior accordingly.

So I tried, and I managed to make some progress. I paid a lot more attention to my inner feelings and thoughts. I started to pay attention to how I would relate to people and how I felt about them. I tried to focus on others and stop paying so much attention to the demons inside. It wasn't easy. It was actually really hard work. Hard work that took a lot out of me, hard work that left me back where I was to begin with. I was so busy fighting against my brain that I had no room to let the good in. There was no space available to fill with joy or happiness. It was all still dark and gloomy, and I couldn't find a way to change that.

Until, one day, I checked Ozzy Osbourne's autobiography out from the library and began to read it. Starting at age 13, he had been one of the biggest influences in my life. I had wanted to be like him. He was able to do all sorts of crazy drugs and drink as much as he wanted, and he did okay. I wanted to be crazy and wild like him. I wanted to drink and drug and have the time of my life like him. Only it didn't work out that way. I wasn't destined to have that kind of life and, over the years, I had moved away from "wanting to be like Ozzy", and on to wanting to live my own life. Or not live it, depending on my mental and emotional state at the time. So when I got to the point in his book where he talked about getting sober, something clicked for me. Here was my childhood idol talking about how his life changed for the better once he got sober. That he had a *lot* of fun while drinking and drugging, but that it was nothing compared to sobriety.

Could that be the answer? I had tried everything *but* getting sober so far, and hadn't made much progress. I mean, I had managed to stop drinking here and there, sometimes for up to a week or so, but I was never really in a place where I could seriously entertain stopping for good. I had too much going on in my head, and I had needed to drown that darkness in something since I had no other way of dealing with it. So was I really ready to take that leap? Could I seriously consider removing alcohol from the equation and then moving forward with healing? I knew that I was pretty much stuck as far as healing went. I knew that the drinking was acting as an anchor and holding me back. I knew that it was adding to my depression and feeding my darkest thoughts. But I also knew where I was, and I was comfortable there. I knew what to expect. To remove that barrier was scary. I had spent 30 years drinking and doing drugs to avoid my feelings. To even consider removing that from the equation was scary. It meant that I was going to have to turn everything upside down and deal with my past on a level that I wasn't sure I was ready for. But, ready or not, I knew it was time. I couldn't move forward the way things were, and I needed to take that next step. I needed to do this for my family. I needed to do this for myself. Besides, if Ozzy could do it, so could I, right?

So, the next morning, I found myself standing at the door to a rehab center.

They couldn't take me right away and told me to come back in two days. I was okay with that, though. In the past, I probably would have taken that as my cue to go back out drinking and not return. After all, if they couldn't take me right then and there, then I wasn't going to bother going back. But, this time, I did go back. The two days gave me time to schedule things with my work. It also gave me time to break the news to my family. They knew it was time for me to stop drinking. They had known for a long time. Even if they had no idea exactly how much I was drinking daily, they knew I was drinking far too much and had come home a couple of times to find me totally wasted – even passed out in the driveway at one point. I felt supported by everybody and I was determined to use this opportunity to change my life.

There have been three times when a decision I made actually made a huge impact on the quality of my life for the long term. The first was joining the U.S. Navy, the second was marrying my third wife, and the third was following through on my rehab visit. I wasn't there long, my insurance company threw me out after five days or so, but I was there long enough to detox, long enough to get my head on straight. I had five days of not worrying about work, not worrying about the family, not having to deal with all of the stress of life. I was able to spend my time really reflecting on what alcohol had been doing to my life, and I didn't like what I saw. My day was filled with class after class of this and that…anger management, stress reduction, drug/alcohol education, group therapy. The group therapy was interesting because I was at a place where I was willing to do anything to get better, and that included talking a little bit about what had happened to me. When it came time to talk about why we were there, most people talked about whatever final incident brought them to rehab, such as a DUI or a fight or whatever. Not me – I blurted out that I had been molested by my father and used alcohol to help me cope with the anger and confusion and shame, and that I drank to avoid dealing with relationships in my life. That I was there to hopefully work on these issues because, until I did, I was at risk of going right back out and drinking.

When I was done, the room was silent. Nobody was expecting such a frank disclosure, not even the group leader, but I didn't care. That *was* the reason I was there and I knew my time there was limited so I wanted to make the most of it. But, apparently, that was a bit more than they were ready to handle. After about five seconds of awkward silence, the group counselor told me that was more than they were prepared to deal with and could we just focus on the alcohol. I thought that was a rather odd thing for him to say, but whatever. I wasn't sure how I was going to be able to fix the one without the other but, as I had so many times before, I decided I just needed to keep the abuse to myself. People really didn't want to hear about it. Not because they weren't fascinated by it, but because they couldn't deal with it. Again I found that those who should have been able to help, who had the training for this sort of thing, didn't want to touch it. It was too intense, it went too deep. While I can see his point – there just wasn't enough time to deal with it while I was there – it, once again, made me feel like I needed to carry this burden alone.

But I needed to share it with somebody. I needed to unload this darkness and shine a light on it. I had found that was the only way to lessen it, the only way to take away its power. But this wasn't the time or the place, apparently. It seemed that nowhere was the "time or the place". I was beginning to wonder if perhaps I was going to just have to suck it up and carry this around with me by myself for the rest of my life.

When my five days was up and I was getting ready to leave, I had my checkout interview. I hadn't been there long enough to really get the full benefit, but I had been there long enough to know that I needed to continue on living what I had learned if I was to get any better. I had gone five days without drinking before, and it wasn't like I was leaving there fresh and free, not wanting to drink because I didn't want to blow five days of sobriety. But I did have a new mindset. I was leaving there with a new way of looking at things. I was leaving there determined to continue healing no matter what it took.

So it kind of pissed me off when, during the exit interview, my counselor told me he believed he would see me again. Soon. He wanted me to stay. He felt that the insurance company was doing me a total disservice by kicking me out. That I needed the full 30 days, that this short of a stay was useless. I had too many issues to deal with and he predicted that I would be drinking again within a month. Didn't he realize that I had worked hard to make the most of my time there? That I had fully participated in every class, every therapy session? That I had taken advantage of everything they had to offer and worked my butt off to make sure this whole thing was not going to be a waste of my time? Screw him. I was determined to prove him wrong. I was a lot stronger than he thought I was. I wasn't the weak person he seemed to believe I was. Sure, there were some pretty big obstacles I would need to overcome, some pretty deep wounds I needed to heal, but who did he think he was passing judgment on me like that? I was ready. I was determined. I was packed and I was pissed.

So home I went.

11

"Help me, tell me I'm sane. I feel a change in the earth, in the wind and the rain."

– Black Sabbath, *Falling Off the Edge of the World*

By now, my dad was dead. He had died a horrible, painful death due to liver failure. My sisters and I visited him on his deathbed to get some closure, and his dying words to me were "I'm sorry you were hurt by what I did". Not "I'm sorry for what I did", but "sorry you were hurt"… if there was ever a non-apology, that was it. But even though it wasn't a true apology, it was something. It made me realize that maybe he didn't really realize the gravity of his behavior. Even though I didn't feel like he had really apologized, I was able to cling to the thought that he was just a sick person that didn't really know better. However, I believe he *did* know better, but he really was pretty sick and twisted and, to him, what he had done wasn't a big deal, just like all those other pedophiles I had tracked and sent to prison. They also believed there was nothing wrong with what they were doing.

But now he was dead. Gone. No longer a threat. While I did feel a small weight lift off my shoulders at his death, nothing really changed. No matter how many times I reminded myself that he was gone, I would still find my heart pounding and my chest tightening when I would see somebody who looked like him walking down the street towards me. No matter how many times I told myself that he couldn't hurt me, I still jumped and lashed out when people touched me unexpectedly. I was your typical, on-edge, PTSD sufferer that seemed to see danger around every corner. But I had been that way for so long that I had pretty much just accepted that was how it was going to be. I had trouble holding conversations with people. Instead of focusing on what they were saying, I found myself constantly scanning the environment. Instead of listening to them, I found myself off somewhere else in my head, thinking about other things. I had trouble relating because I had no focus. I was good at making people think I was listening, though. I nodded and said "right" or "uh-huh" at the correct times, but I wasn't listening at all. I could have entire conversations with people and have no idea what we talked about.

My amygdala was in overdrive without the alcohol to quiet it. I'm not a scientist, but I have learned that one of basic roles of the amygdala is to form and store memories of emotional events, making it the "home" for all of the horrible memories I had as a child. The problem with the amygdala is that it doesn't recognize time and/or space. Because its function is to keep you safe, it stores those memories and you are able to recall them just as you did when you were experiencing them for the first time. It provides a sense of urgency when you're experiencing something that was dangerous once before. For example, if you burn your foot on a floor heater when you're four (as I did), your amygdala will store that painful memory. 20 years later, when you're about to step on another floor heater, your amygdala will release that memory as if it was fresh and remind you just how painful that was. This would explain why I would have panic attacks whenever I would see somebody who looked like my father approaching me. My amygdala was flooding my brain with warning signals.

So how do you change that? How can you change your memories? They are what they are, and you can't erase them from your mind.

So I kept reading, and researching, and talking with other parents who had children with trauma backgrounds. I started blogging about my adventures and found that to be somewhat therapeutic. Much like writing this book, as I put my thoughts to paper, I began to see things differently and that allowed me to step back and think about them. I also kept pushing ahead with making sure my daughter had what she needed to succeed, and that involved quite a bit of dealing with the school district, sometimes to the point of making demands and finding the solutions myself before presenting them. Basically, I was telling them where we needed to be and what steps we needed to take to get there, then letting them fill in the details. I wasn't taking "no" for an answer, and it worked... but it worked in a way I hadn't imagined. Yes, we got my daughter everything she needed to help her succeed (she finished her final semester of her senior year in high school with a GPA of 3.4) but, somewhere along the way, I began to find myself feeling a little less stressed out. Granted, I was still *very* stressed and on-edge all the time, but it didn't have that punishing, heavy, crushing feeling that I was used to. I was finding that the more energy I focused on somebody else, the less energy I had to use worrying about my own emotional and mental state. Nothing was really changing. I was still on-edge and couldn't have people touch me unexpectedly or be in an elevator with somebody who resembled my father without my blood pressure spiking and my chest tightening, but there was just something that felt good about being able to do something for somebody else, being able to fight for something that I believed in. I found that I loved that fight. I loved having a "cause".

That isn't to say my life was noticeably changing, though. I was still trudging through life, going to work, trying to focus on getting sober and dealing with all of the things that were new to me as a result. Honestly, I guess I expected some sort of incredible life-changing something or other to wash over me and make everything all better, but it didn't happen. However, after about four months of being sober, I noticed something. Something different. Something I realized I had never been able to do.

I could look at myself in the mirror and be okay with what I saw.

Sure, I had been able to look at myself in the mirror before, but I never really looked myself in the eyes. I had too much shame, too much embarrassment over what had happened. I didn't really like myself and was ashamed of what I had allowed to happen. I had "accepted" what had happened. Intellectually, I had come to terms with it. After all, it had happened and nothing could change that, but that didn't mean I was okay with it…not on an emotional level. To look myself in the eyes was to see all that sadness and hurt so I just didn't do it. I *couldn't* do it.

But one day I could. One day I looked myself in the eyes and I was okay with the person looking back at me. I was reminded of one night while living in my grandparent's house, sleeping in the room my grandfather had died in. I had woken up in the middle of the night and sat up in bed. There was my grandfather at the foot of the bed, and all he said was "It will be alright", then he was gone. Was it just a dream? A ghostly visit? I don't know. I will never know for sure, I suppose, but the message was clear; "It will be alright". I clung to that message for years, drawing hope and inspiration from it, but never knowing really what he meant. *When* would it be "alright"? What was he talking about? That day, looking at myself in the mirror, it began to hit home. Maybe it really *was* going to be alright.

Slowly things continued to get better. I continued to remain sober, my daughter was healing, I was healing. Or was I? Sure, I was starting to feel better. I was feeling less depressed all the time, less anxious and angry. But I still couldn't cry, no matter how I tried. I still wasn't a very "loving" person. It was effort for me to hug anybody, including my own daughters, and it didn't feel comfortable. I didn't like being close to people, physically or emotionally, so I remained offish and cold. Not drinking wasn't really helping with that, either. It wasn't making it worse, but it *was* making me see it more, and that made me sad. I still wasn't the type of parent I wanted to be, that my children deserved. They needed somebody who would scoop them up and tell them how much they were loved. They needed a father who could sit and have tea with them without going somewhere else in his mind. Somebody who could focus on them and their lives, who could listen and empathize and stroke their hair when they were sad and upset, telling them it will be alright.

But I couldn't be that person. I wanted to be, but that wasn't enough. I would try, but it was uncomfortable, awkward, and felt completely unnatural. Just being sober wasn't really changing me and helping me become the person I really felt I could, and should, be. What it *was* doing was letting me see all of my flaws, all of my shortcomings, all of the ways I wished I could be different. But as for helping me get there? It wasn't cutting it. My children were growing up and I was missing it all. I was stuck in a rut that I just couldn't figure out how to escape from it. I wanted something different. I needed more of a boost to really jump start the healing. I needed to really mix things up.

Then I found it.

I enjoyed the job I was doing at the time. I had my own office, I had plenty of freedom to do things my way, and lots of downtime to relax. But, like everything else, it was routine and I didn't feel I was making enough money so I looked around and found something else. It was perfect for me, and it was literally a thousand miles away. It was an opportunity to start fresh, to start over, to start anew.

So we moved.

Because of the job change, I lost my health insurance. As a result, I decided to go off my anti-depressants. My wife was complaining that they made me too "robotic" anyway so it seemed like a good decision to just give them up. After all, I was in a new place, with new people and a new job. It was a gamble for sure, but one I felt I was willing to take. I decided I would replace my medication with meditation, something I had been doing on and off for a while, but never seriously got into it. It was really difficult, though. Sitting there, trying to quiet my racing thoughts wasn't easy but, slowly, I got better at it and the more I was able to do it, the more I didn't want to stop. The peace and calm it brought on was addictive. I seemed to be more able to handle the stresses that came at me each day, but no matter how calm it made me, it did nothing to address the darkness that I still carried around in my soul. The bleak hopelessness I sometimes felt, the overwhelming disgust and shame over what had happened. It was all still there, waiting to drag me back down like a hungry demon. I found I was fine as long as I didn't dredge up any memories or thoughts of the things my father had done, but there were always little things that would set me off. My daughters would do or say something, or I would see somebody on the street that looked like my father. I found there were times I would just have to pull over while driving and just sit there until it passed. The past still had a hold on me and I couldn't break it no matter what I tried.

About a year after the move, my wife and I decided to take our daughter to a therapist who specialized in trauma history. She had been carrying around a ton of anger because of the fact that I had moved out not once, but twice. And no matter how hard I tried, we just couldn't seem to bond and every time we fought, I cursed my father even more. What he had done didn't just affect me, but my children, and I was still afraid that it would affect *their* children. Childhood abuse creates lifelong problems that go far beyond just the person that was abused, and that wasn't fair. It wasn't fair to my wife, and it certainly wasn't fair to my daughters. They hadn't done anything, yet they were having to live with the fallout.

One of the things this new therapist specialized in was EMDR (Eye Movement Desensitization and Reprocessing) and Lifespan Integration therapies. We ended up taking both of my daughters to see her, and after I chatted with her about those particular therapeutic techniques, I began to wonder if they might work for me.

So I scheduled an appointment.

I wasn't particularly interested in the EMDR. To me, it seemed silly…using eye movements to help the amygdala process the memories and remove them from the "here and now". I was more interested in the Lifespan Integration. In a nutshell, the LI was designed to help "retrain" the amygdala by activating the neural pathways that were associated with a particular memory, then moving forward through time by going through memories a year at a time until you reach your current age. This "teaches" the brain that what happened did so a long time ago and is no longer a threat. It was a relatively new therapy, about eight-years-old, which had been successfully used on people with trauma history. I saw that it seemed to be making a difference in my daughter so I agreed to give it a try.

Even though it sounds simple enough, it isn't easy, especially with a complex trauma history such as mine. I had to give the therapist a list of memories – one for each year beginning at age five. That wasn't easy with several years being almost completely blacked out, but we managed to put it together and I went in for my first LI session.

She had me "activate" those memories, which instantly flooded me with anxiety and stress. I couldn't do this. Having to vividly remember what happened that first time caused my body to physically recoil. My chest was tightening up, my head was throbbing, my throat was closing up, and I had to consciously remind myself to breathe. I wanted to put all of this behind me, but this was too much. I wanted to curl up and disappear. I didn't want to do this. It was torture. It seemed that it would be easier to just leave things alone and live with the darkness.

We went through that one memory about five times, each time I wondered why I was putting myself through it. Each time we started and I activated the memory, I felt like I was going to explode. I didn't want to be there. But each time we went through it, it got a little easier. Each time the memory seemed to lose a little of its power over me.

When we were done, I was physically, emotionally, and mentally drained. I walked to the car like a zombie. I sat there behind the wheel wondering what the hell had just happened. I wasn't sure if I felt good or bad. I didn't know if I was pleased or unhappy. I couldn't think. I couldn't drive so I just sat there for a good 15 minutes until I felt I was okay to leave. Then I went home and just laid on the couch for an hour or so. I didn't know what had just happened to me and I wasn't sure I wanted to do it again.

But I went back the next week. I said I wanted to try the EMDR since the LI was far too intense. I couldn't handle that on a regular basis. It *did* have a positive effect on me, though. Something about me felt different. I felt lighter. I felt slightly more in control of myself. But the shame and confusion and anger were all still there.

So we tried the EMDR. We worked on the same memory since it continued to haunt me…that first time he said "Let's play" and had me remove my clothes. That bright, sunny day with the floral bedspread and the light blue pillowcases. That day that changed my life. We spent the entire hour doing the EMDR session and it seemed to help, and it wasn't nearly as intense. But it was almost too easy. If you imagine the trauma as a gaping, infected wound filled with pus, the EMDR was similar to tearing off the bandage and letting it heal over. It was effective, but slow. In contrast, the LI was more akin to not just ripping off the bandage, but scooping out all the pus and infection with a spoon and throwing it away before allowing it to heal over. Psychically, it was incredibly painful, but effective. Both methods seemed to be effective, but I wanted this to be over. I didn't want to take things slowly. I didn't want to be haunted by this for years to come. I had again opened Pandora's Box, and I wasn't willing to shut it until it was empty.

So I scheduled another LI.

12

"Of all the things I value most of all, I look inside myself and see my world, and know that it is good."

– Black Sabbath, *Spiral Architect*

I had reached the point where I was okay talking about the abuse. I was finding that the more I talked about it, the less power it had over me, and I liked that feeling. I wasn't quite ready to talk about it with the people that were closest to me, but people I didn't know well and who didn't really know me were safe. Even though I knew now that it wasn't my fault, that there wasn't anything I could have really done about it, there was still too much shame and embarrassment to discuss it with people I wanted to like me. I was afraid people would think less of me so I stuck to people that I wasn't close to, but I found that people didn't want to hear about it.

I found that for most people, it's too tragic, too sad. Child abuse is still one of those subjects that makes people uneasy, and many act as though they don't know what to do if you bring it up. It is a conversation stopper in most cases so I fought the urge and tried to only bring it up when I felt it was already the subject. I wouldn't give details, but I was able to say "I was abused by my father". But even that caused most people to shrink away. They just didn't want to talk about such things.

But almost invariably, when I would mention something in a social setting such as Facebook, I would get a message from somebody telling me that they, too, had been abused. I began to hear the horror stories that others had been hiding down deep inside them. The stories that had changed their lives in the same way mine had.

I've read the statistics. 1 in 4 women and 1 in 6 men are thought to have been sexually abused to some degree, but those are just numbers. Numbers are safe. Numbers don't mean much. But I was beginning to put faces to those numbers. Some people I had known since childhood and never, ever had a clue of the horrors they were going through. Others I had just met. Like me, those people seemed to find it easier to speak with somebody they weren't close to. Like me, those people had some horrific stories to tell that shocked and saddened me. Like me, those people had their lives completely changed by what had happened.

Unlike me, they were all women. As of this writing, not a single male has come forward and told me his story. I know they are out there. I've seen the books written for male survivors of sexual abuse, although when I did a quick search for support groups in my area for survivors of sexual abuse, I found two – both for women. There is still a social stigma to being a man that is a victim of sexual abuse. I feel it. I know that to be a man in this society means you are expected to be powerful, commanding, dominant. You are allowed to have feelings, even show them. In fact, it's taken as a positive sign when you are able to show feelings, even fear to some extent. But not really. That is acceptable around women, but not other men. And to whine around other guys about how you were a victim is easily one of the biggest no-no's. It instantly puts you in a position of submission. After all, you allowed yourself to be a victim. You lose all your "man points". Even though you aren't "whining" about it, that's how many people seem to see it. You can talk about how your little league team lost every game, or how you never got the "hot girl" in high school. You can talk about how your car broke down and left you stranded somewhere, or how the vacation you planned was completely rained out. Those are okay, but if you talk about how you were sexually or physically abused, it becomes "whining". This is, I suspect, why many men don't come forward. We aren't whiners, we aren't weak, and we aren't less of a man for having been abused. But society has taught us that we will be seen that way when we come forward so we don't. There are few support groups where we can meet other victims. There are places online where people gather but, as with any other online group, there are trolls, there are people who aren't there to heal but to cause problems, there are people who would make you feel less of a person in order to boost themselves up. These aren't the most healing of environments so we go it alone.

And for those of us who choose to take the path of healing, both men and women, we find that the rewards are huge. At least for me, working through the fear of "what's next" is a huge part. Many times during my journey, I wanted to stop. I was no longer living under that black cloud that haunted me throughout my life. Sure, I hadn't found the sun yet, but I was feeling freer, more open, more alive than I ever had before. When I looked back, I would see the wreckage of the past falling away. It was a great place to be. But I knew I had further to go, that my journey wasn't over.

Looking forward, all I could see was more hard work. At times, I wondered whether it would be worth continuing with all that hard work. Why couldn't I just stay where I was? After all, I was in a far better place than I used to be, and had no idea what lie ahead. Love? I got it, but was there more to it? What was hiding behind that wall ahead? If I smashed through it, would it be worth the work? Would things be even better than they were? I had no idea, and it was scary…scary to wonder what lie ahead. As strange as it sounds, for things to get better was a frightening thought. I had spent so long living in the darkness that I had no idea what life could be like without it. I had no clue whether I could handle the emotions, the drama, the filling light of life. It was unknown, and the unknown is scary.

But I press forward. I wanted to know what was out there. I wasn't satisfied with sitting in the shadows any longer. I wanted to love, to laugh. I wanted to feel what it was like to connect to another human being without any sexual undertones. I wanted to live.

I continued to re-visit the darkest places of my mind. I forced myself to relive them in order to show my subconscious that they were no longer a threat, that all the horror and confusion happened long ago, that today was a new day. I continued to force myself to focus on other people, to share in their joys and their pain. In my head, I practiced what it would be like to hold my daughters without stiffening up, to truly be there for them in their times of need. I stopped trying to hold back my emotions out of fear, and just tried to let them flow free.

I went in, week after week, beating up the past and healing the future. One week, I just let my anger flow and, in my head, beat up my father. It was horrible. As part of the therapy, I had to take myself back to a particular incident and then "walk in" as my adult self and "rescue" my eleven-year-old self. But I couldn't just take him away. I had to show him my adult self could protect him so I started punching my father over and over, harder and harder. All of the anger, the confusion, the hate, and the love flowed out. It was quite easily one of the most intense things I have ever experienced. Years of suffocating under his dominance fell away; with every punch, his power over me grew less and less. I had the power now. I had the power and I hated what he did. I hated the way he ruined my life. I hated the way he ruined my children's lives. I hated him so much that I wanted to beat him into a bloody pulp, and when I was done, I was physically exhausted. I couldn't move. I just sat there, wondering where that had come from. I didn't feel any better. I actually felt worse. As much as I hated him, I loved him for his good qualities. I didn't feel bad about beating him up, but I felt confused and conflicted.

But over the next couple of days I found that his power over me was hugely diminished. Before, when I would think back to that particular incident of sexual depravity, my body would react. I would feel myself tensing up and all those stress hormones would flow and get my body ready for fight or flight. I would get a headache or my throat would close up. I would have the urge to curl into a ball and disappear.

But no longer. Now I was able to see it as something that happened a long time ago, something that was no longer a threat but just a memory. Much like losing a little league game or having my car break down, it was just something that happened in the past.

As abuse victims, we hear all the time that "You need to get over it", or "You need to move past it". It isn't that simple. People mean well, but they have no idea just how difficult it is to get to that point. How painful it is, how much work is involved. People have the best intentions, but they just don't understand. If you haven't lived it, if you haven't experienced it, your brain doesn't work the same way ours does. If your dog dies when you're 30, you can "get over it". If a parent dies when you're 40, you eventually can "move past it". Don't get me wrong. This isn't to say people who lose pets and parents don't suffer. You most certainly do, but it's different. When you live through seriously traumatic events at a young age, your brain goes into survival mode and sticks there. Imagine your worst fear, then think about what it would be like to live with that day after day, never knowing when it was going to happen, only that it will. You know it is going to happen at any time, but there is nothing you can do about it. Think about how that would mess with your mind. Abuse victims can't talk themselves into changing that. No matter how many happy little stories you tell them, no matter how many positive, life-affirming memes you post for them on Facebook or how many times you tell them you love them, they aren't going to "just get over it". In fact, I found that reading all of those memes that people post just made me feel worse. I *wanted* to "just get over it". I *wanted* to follow those "10 things to make you happy". I knew those things could work. I just couldn't get myself to a place where they would. That isn't to say you can't help. You can be understanding, you can be supportive, you can realize we come from a different place in our heads. But you can't change us. Only we can do that.

That also isn't to say you should stop posting your memes, or that you should give up wanting the best for us, but you can't dismiss our pain and horror by telling us to "Just get over it already". It doesn't work. In fact, it has the opposite effect. You will end up becoming one of those people we don't go to for support because you obviously have no clue.

As for me, I suspect that I still have a long way to go. I feel blessed that I found my path to healing, and wish I had found it sooner. I look back on my life and see how it has affected every aspect of living, from relationships to caring about myself to the type of person I grew up to be. I see how I dragged the darkness along with me and cast that shadow over everybody I met and cared about. I see how it had a negative impact on my children and I hope they can heal, as well. But I also see the light ahead. I can finally allow myself to appreciate the happiness in others. I can allow myself to be me. I can love.

In fact, my youngest daughter just recently had her heart broken. Rather than blowing it off as just more teenage drama, like I would have done in the past because emotions are just too hard to deal with, I was able to reach out, pull her towards me, and just hold her while she cried. I didn't cry, but I was close. I could feel, I could empathize, I could love.

It's a journey that has been hard going, more painful than I could have imagined, but the rewards have been worth it. I'm not there yet, but I realized one thing as I was holding my heartbroken, crying daughter. My grandfather was right.

It'll be alright.

Made in the USA
San Bernardino, CA
05 May 2014